The Creature

Kameron Price

ISBN 978-1-105-62084-3

Dedicated to all those
affected
by the "butterfly"

- C o n t e n t s -

A. Preface   (pages 1-8)

*Manursive & The Matrix

B. The Synthesis of the Archives   (pages 9-60)

*Created Concepts

*The Tempest Sea of Culture

*Of Masks & Masochism

*The Feeble Safeguards of Longevity

*The Cauldron of Scientific Entities

C. Purpose Decay   (pages 61-118)

*Teleologically Thwarted Legacy

*Dissonant Moral Architecture

*The Evolved Predator Mechanisms that Usurp

D. Nascent Omniscience   (pages 119-134)

*Utopian Insights & Further Questioning

E. Epilogue   (pages 135-142)

*Redundant Manifestations

F. Credits   (pages 143-158)

G. Index   (pages 159-160)

P r e f a c e

---Manursive & The Matrix---

"Every mammal on this planet instinctively develops a natural equilibrium with the surrounding environment but you humans do not. You move to an area and you multiply and multiply until every natural resource is consumed and the only way you can survive is to spread to another area. There is another organism on this planet that follows the same pattern. Do you know what it is? A virus. Human beings are a disease, a cancer of this planet." -The Matrix(1999)[1]

Being the recluse yet anti-religious (the most of which accounted for my rebellious stage) teenager that I was, on top of a slight relationship mishap, I discovered philosophy and all other -ologies where fascinating and due to my brains' plasticity it all unleashed a creative surge starting my junior year of high school. I can't remember when exactly but at some point I had viewed The Matrix and was bewildered. Moreover, I was a typical teenager in the sense that I was just starting to get a clue about the world around me, so all the movies

and ideas my friends had seen had synthe-
sized in me and I started writing poetry
with a verbose technical edge.

A couple friends and I had musical
instruments at the time and always toyed
with the idea of starting a band. What else
would friends do in this situation? So we
did.

At first we just got together and had
fun making noise in my parents' basement. As
a few weeks passed we got the idea to put
words to our amalgam of house shaking fre-
quencies. Our first song was "Candid" and as
it happened I was the only one that had
lyric-type material available so we tried
them out.

I would like to over zealously bolster
my ego by saying that my way with words at
the time were superior to anyone else's,
among us three guys or anyone around us with
the same ideas of being in a band, but modestly I think it just happened that I spewed
out lyrics that fit whereas the other two
created riffs and melodies.

I look back at those poems, most of
which were incorporated into songs for
Manursive, and I still don't quite understand what I was saying because at the time
I wanted lyrics that one had to get a dictionary out to define and decode what was

being imparted.

One of our songs I actually co-wrote because the guitar player (Matt Lorenz) couldn't quite get into words what he wanted to say. This became "Lunar Abyss" which was song three I believe.

Our second song was "For How" and I was inspired to write those lyrics after watching the movie Blow. The bass/ singer (Chris Curtis) had to question me many times with those lyrics because parts were just nonsensical verbiage. This incident lead to an inside joke about the use of the word "indeed". The original lyrics were likened to Boston's "Peace of Mind" but in them I said something like "for how, indeed, am I to live in a kingdom of competition." Eventually I revamped the whole song. I even remember rewriting the intro after I burned my hand on a grill at work.

As our workings continued as three high schoolers spending afternoons and weekends jamming out in our fog-filled, strobe light pulsating, rock-star wannabe basement, we eventually came up with eight songs to record. Coinciding with our efforts I was having a friend from school (Megan Ketcham) draw some artwork for our album. One day she showed me a drawing of a bee-like creature with a skull head and I remember being in awe and wanted more. So I told her to exper-

iment with those creatures in a scene. What
she produced became our artwork for our
poster and our liner notes. She also let us
use another drawing of a hand with a spider-
web for the back of the album. Chris was the
one who christened the album <u>OmniNecroVore</u>
and thus our baby was born.

Metaphorically eating everything that
is dead (which is what omninecrovore means)
references the usage of concepts or inventions that were in existence before that are
now being built upon. This complex metaphor
always inspired me in fact its incorporated
into the lyrics of the song "The Creature".
The last verse goes:

> All has been dead and will be devoured again
> Failing all respect for self
> This fauna is a vex upon all hope of survival
> With no barrier to secure our vitality

I also used this idea in our instrumental
track called "The All Saints Church of
Sedlec" which was inspired by Metallica's
"To live is to Die":

> Exhumed from our innocence
> Will be our remnants
> In the history to come

Ironically, the All Saints Church of Sedlec
is a real church in the Czech Republic that
used the bones of 40,000 people to decorate
the chapel.[2]

Anyway, another recurring theme in my

lyrics on <u>OmniNecroVore</u> reference the quote at the beginning of this chapter. In The Matrix the antagonist machines categorize humans as a cancer of the planet and fervently want to be the cure. I ruminated on this idea for some time and incorporated it into many lines, including:

From "Nothing is Sacred" -

Defiled Earth to fit our need
Molded landscape is our change
Custom nature will always be
Evolution with no harmony

And from "Lunar Abyss" -

Chaos will reign
To relieve the terrestrial burden
So unconscious, gullible
A fatal scar by mortals

The aforementioned last verse of "The Creature" also uses this theme.

I can't account for what the other members of Manursive thought about my lyrics, or what I was aiming for with lyrics that were yet to be put to music, but for me I always wanted to make heavy metal philosophical. And actually there are a few metal examples of what I was aiming for. These albums, for example, are classified under progressive metal, but fit with my notion of a philosophy based genre: Arcturus' "Sham Mirrors", Winds' "Reflections of the I", The Kovenant's "S.E.T.I.", Vintersorg's "Cosmic

Genesis", and Pagan's Mind's "God's Equation". These, among others I'm sure, are trying different song structures and lyrical arrangements. There is also a metal subgenre called grindcore that mixes impor- tant ideas with metal. Ultimately, the occa- sional questioning of existence is sure to inhabit all music since all music is made from a species who questions. I say this only to point out redundancy, which I will explore later.

Moving on, I was always disappointed by lyrics from people that were full of teenage angst and curse words. Reading lyrics about a lost girlfriend or about hating the gov- ernment or about the pleasures of sex was boring, especially if the vocabulary was dull. This all simply implied a lack of artistry to me. Another thing that was annoying (and still sometimes is) is when professional musicians improvise their lyrics as they make their music. Cradle of Filth is one example of a band whose lyrics are always above and beyond the norm. Dani Filth always uses arcane vocabulary and sin- ister prose to express some gothic tale. I, like Dani, put thought into my lyrics and always thought that lyrical content was an art too although my lyrics are no match for the level of Dani's.

Back when Manursive still had jam sessions, I had visions of expressing some philosophical story through future lyrics (and I had numerous other poem like lyrics in cache) but time and creative differences didn't allow that to happen. Here it is eight years later and I am just now deciding to turn all my lyrical ideas and other writing into a philosophical treatise. In fact, at least as early as 2002 I've had ideas for this writing project. I remember fantasizing about writing a book or a doctoral dissertation long before I had even graduated high school. I was slightly self-righteous back then. I guess I still am but now I've refined my thoughts and I've become more stoic. What's more, I always associated the artwork of <u>OmniNecroVore</u> as a representation of my lyrics. The ubiquitous and ominous bee like creatures of the album began to symbolize in my mind the anomaly of nature known as the human. The omnipresence of humans and their products convey their horrific and egotistical behavior. Their images contain gnarled histories of flowing blood, viciousness, apathetic tendencies, bias, herd like behavior, and vain scavenger frenzy. To remind the reader of such mannerisms I'm including the creature graphic to open each chapter.

Throughout these pages I will be exploring numerous social, political, and

scientific finding and relating them to my
observation of humanity. Since I'm referencing a catalogue of human knowledge most
of what I'm saying here will be redundant.
That's not to say that reading this will be
the first time you will encounter such a
collection of ideas, but rather that in general such ideas have been explored before
and are being explored everyday by every
person. Just take a college philosophy
class and you will learn a plethora of
counter ideas to every idea that has ever
existed. Furthermore, there are scientists,
ecologists, meterologists, biologists, cosmologists, theologians, mathematicians, historians, environmentalists, sociologists,
anthropologists, etc. that are researching
the very ideas I will recount in this piece,
and that are also postulating things that
I'm not even aware of or can even fathom.
Basically, the network of human imagination
and concern (and the fact that humans have
tons of free time and specialized careers
that are tailored to engage in research)
will always infiltrate the archives of
humanity with ideas about their findings..

The Synthesis
of the Archives

---Created Concepts---

As a thought experiment pretend you are just a pair of eyes. No language and no understanding of the world. Just an observer. For the sake of argument you can speak about what you see but you can only question what you see.

For example, there is a couple kissing romantically let's say in a city park and there are numerous other people around enjoying summer activities. Well: what is kissing? Where did these people come from? Why are only the people covered but not other animals? Moreover, what's under the clothes? Why does one set of people have long strands of hair and others have short hair? What are all these people thinking about at this moment? Why are people different heights? Why aren't other people engaging in the act that this couple is? Why do some people have different colored bodies?

If this exercise was taken to any envi-

ronment one would notice that everything
around us is human made, understood, and
artificial. Landscapes molded at whim,
architecture for decoration and efficiency,
sewers to transport waste, road systems,
city planning, markets of all types, sciences of all types, art, music, literature,
norms of culture, clothes, gender stereotypes, racial stereotypes, love, hate, language, government, control, etc. Even nomenclature is something humans have invented to
maximize the efficiency of communication, so
naming and categorizing things is very much
a part of human-ness. Take for example the
taxonomic rank of humans: animalia (kingdom), chordata (phylum), mammalia (class),
primates (order), hominidae (family), homo
(genus), and homo sapiens (species).[1] In
addition, geologists classify time into eras
and epochs. We are currently in the Holocene
epoch of the Quaternary period, of the
Cenozoic era, of the Phanerozoic eon.[2]
Labeling is also a means of segregation. A
word may be just a word but some words have
weight and are used in a derogatory way to
degrade things or people.

Holidays, too, are just a means of cel-
ebration. Most holidays are celebrated without any knowledge of its origins. Holidays
to me are just an excuse to party and spend
money.

Since humans have a complex linguistic side, the very act of me typing out letters to form words and sentences by following rules of grammar is ultimately only understood by other humans who have completed primary education and thus are able to understand said linguistic rules.

Justice, choice, equality, liberty, and citizenship are also concepts and fall under the category of politics. Philosophy is politics in action (I will discuss the evolution and foundation of philosophy in "The Tempest sea of Culture"). As groups accumulated and formed societies governments of control have formed. It has been, after centuries of redundant squabbling, that America itself was founded under Enlightenment humanitarian concepts. These of which were created in reaction to scientific discoveries, optimism, and European turmoil starting in the late 1600s.[3] Ideas about social contract, human nature, and civic rights came from such thinkers as Denis Diderot, Thomas Hobbes, John Locke, and Jean-Jacques Rousseau which inspired and paved the path for the most powerful and free country in the world.[4] Unfortunately, and this is a dark reality, colonization, exploitation and vicious political strategy have transformed the U.S. into such a super power that all the world not only envies but also begrudges.

I'm personally contemptuous of being a white human American male for all the notoriety those four elements contain. It's a bold statement I know but think about it: being human comprises of speciesist actions towards other animals, anthropocentrism, and human error; being white comes with the history of exploiting other races; males are infamous for sexism and patriarchy; and Americans (although safe, secure, and full of luxuries) have a history of slavery, killing off Native peoples with diseases and advanced weaponry, and vain involvement in world wars. Jared Diamond's book <u>Guns, Germs, and Steel</u>[5] talks about such behavior and how it relates to how the Western world was created. All in all, my four loathsome points are the most advantageous, the most notoriously destructive, and the most historically baneful. If one is born with all these elements they automatically exist on a level higher than anyone who has only a couple of these elements.

I digress. Moving on. Meaning is also a concept (I will talk briefly of meaning in "Of Masks & Masochism). Only humans bequeath meaning; thus the meaning of life is a concept only humans can understand. Do you think lower animals question their reality? No, because their brains aren't as advanced

as ours. Since the advent of encephaliza-
tion and eventual bipedialism in hominids
creativity has exploded. This creativity is
a result of synaptic and chemical induced
activity in the brain. And as such, humans
have fabricated an un-natural habitat for
themselves. We are controlled by nature but
live in a self created world.

Due to anthropocentric tendencies,
humans have a morbid fear of their own mortality so to question life's purpose is to
quench and suppress any horrors of a world
devoid of the human ego. What's more, existence (being conscious of oneself) is a
human concept used to question our cognizance and our trajectory into the future.
This fear of the unknown is a direct result
of over protection and violence for sometimes unnecessary actions. People tend to
act hastily when faced with fear and have
been known to kill over it. Dissent seems
to be a form of fear as well.

So much of the human condition consists
merely of products of fear toward the
unknown just because our brains won't stop
thinking. In fact, it's he superfluity of
fascinations into the paranormal and mysti-
cal realms (i.e. UFOs, astrology, tarot,
psychics, palmistry, phrenology, astral pro-
jection, numerology, and other transcendent
sports into the metaphysical) that demon-

strates just how far human creativity will go in an effort to find meaning.

Intrinsically, the human brain is constructed of a labyrinth of neural pathways set to electricity. It's through years of family, peer, and environmental conditioning that culminates in an entity called "self". Its been a recurring reflection of mine that I don't really exist due to such psychological findings, and here's why:

1. My body is made of genes from my parents(and their parents ad infinitum).

2. I'm alive due to my hearts electronic pulse.

3. My so-called personality is really a collection of every element of the world, every thought, every pre-natal act from my parents, and every piece of conditioning I've ever experienced.

4. My body is governed by cells that strive for self preservation, ergo every act of nourishment is on some level involuntary.

5. Aside from my personality, my knowledge is based on genetic dispositions and developmental training.

What is this thing called "self"? Why am I an "I"? I'm the only one in all of existence that thinks and feels what I think and feel. This line of questioning leads me to the occasional solipsistic view and in turn supplies a catharsis for the stresses of human interaction.

Fundamentally, you and I are a result from eons of stimulated nervous progressions electrified so intensely that we are able construct a network of communicational devices to understand ourselves and others.

It is our electric bodies that in fact produce the dreams that we so cherish while we sleep. The activation-synthesis theory states that the brain is just making sense of stimulation to the nervous system that renders dreams nothing more.[6] Unlike Sigmund Freud who advocated psychoanalysis to decode dreams as a visual into the subconscious.[7]

Given those points of reference, I've also concluded that "God" is a concept too. Obviously "God" is something everyone says can only be experienced hence making such an understanding purely subjective, but one thing to note is that other animals don't worship anything like humans do. I will explore this topic later in further detail in "Dissonant Moral Architecture".

Ninian Smart was, among other things, an investigator of religions, and concluded that religions include six dimensions: doc-trine, experience, myth, ritual, morality, and organization.[8] Do you ever see lower animals engaged in such activities? No! This leads me to conclude that religion and "God" is only understood through the human mind.

As blasphemous as this all sounds its not because what I am saying is that meaning, belief, possessiveness, and opinions are a result of human imagination and fundamentally don't exist externally and objectively of humanity's grip, so blasphemy is just an idea spawned from human imagination. As long as the human brain can construct imaginative ideas to control and mold the world then concepts will always exist to enlighten us. However, such concepts are just extensions of human cognizance and ego.

When I think of all the strife to defend personal opinions and concepts I just tell myself that everything came from nothing and to nothing it will return. At one point all the fabrications of the human condition, and life itself, didn't exist and at one point everything will cease, especially once there aren't any human minds to comprehend anything of yore.

It is comforting to think that if all matter is made of atoms then the sum of all comprehendable history can be reduced to the colliding of atomic particles. In essence, these particles all have a different valence of electrons that, mixed with the number of neutrons and protons, have resulted, after eons of mixtures, into a complex amalgam of mutant lifeforms that think arrogantly of themselves. And yet out of this aged science

project has spawned ideas that are killed
over.

If existence is just energy then there
surely isn't a Higher Being judging or
directing morality. I mean, the atoms that
make up our bodies, the materials around us,
other animals, and plants are trillions of
years old and are recycled every minute.
When we die we just stop existing in our
current form but what's dead is just our
understanding of the complex life known as a
human. Eating animals, destroying the environment, killing each other, polluting the
atmosphere, and sharing dialogue are all
just a transference of energy. We humans
just hold our complexity in such high regard
due to our sentience that we value everything in terms of right and wrong. For all
eternity energy has swirled around in a
maelstrom of randomness, so suffice it to
say that us humans read too much into life
and all its forms.

People tend to hide behind their
thoughts to carve out individuality. With
everyone battling for their self-righteous
opinions how can any one idea be correct?
In addition, society is so bloated with different options to choose from that no one
knows what to defend. With so many ideas
rampant in the world ideals aren't upheld
and thus fall between the cracks. Such lost

behavior can lead to nihilism.

When it comes down to it there are so many devices that entertain, pleasures to seek, bias traditions to uphold, business endeavors to engage in, and so many peoples' minds to manipulate for greed that I've concluded that the only pleasure in this world is to receive pleasure. However, I'm not a hedonist as I will explain later, rather I'm just saying that we are slaves to our neural activity which renders us unintelligible to our actions. In other words, whatever our brain thinks is pleasurable is what we will yearn for. This phenomenon is an ethical issue when faced with human rights and social control because what is perceived by the cacophony of individual synaptic impulses in the brain causes a different understanding and value of life.

In sum, it's the world and cosmos, in all its beauty and pristine glory, that mystifies our brains and makes the visuals of landscapes seem idyllic and romantic, but if not for our complex society full of technology and concepts we wouldn't be able to comprehend and label everything or become self absorbed in contemplation over existence...

- - - The Tempest Sea of Culture- - -

Culture is basically defined as the set of shared symbols, ideas, and materials products that construct a social system.[1] In such there can be sub cultures of umbrella cultures. For example, any group that shares a perspective can be defined as a culture(i.e. "gay culture").[2] Primarily, though, there exists individualistic and collectivist cultures. Individualist being self focused whereas collectivist means to focus on the group instead. Most philosophers and anthropologists agree that culture is the direct mechanism which elevates humans above mere animals, makes them civilized, and gives breadth to existence. Without culture humans wouldn't have art, music, literature, religion, control, or knowledge. Various forms of these characteristics not only manipulate people but altogether thwart mental enrichment. Ethnocentrism (the term used to characterize prejudice toward different cultures) and political mainframes, for instance, tend to permeate culture for power and phantom agendas resulting in confused and manipulated people. Moreover, these generally make people oblivious to how culture forms their thoughts and daily activities. These upcoming pages are going to include my misan-

thropic thoughts on such power structures
and norms and hopefully impart a new perspective that will unshackle culture's
chains.

It's hard to pinpoint exactly when culture started but archeologists estimate that
shortly after 10,000 BCE, humans began the
systematic husbandry of plants and animals.[3]
These people are classified as being
Neolithic, or a part of the New Stone Age.[4]
Those civilizations that adopted agriculture
had increased stability and productivity
provided by farming and allowed the population to expand.[5] Surplus food allowed a
priestly or governing class to arise followed by a division of labor. The invention
of writing enabled complex societies to
arise. Record-keeping and libraries began
and served as a storehouse of knowledge and
increased the cultural transmission of
information.[6] Furthermore, curiosity and
education drove the pursuit of knowledge and
wisdom. Based on all this I've concluded
that philosophy is atavistic of Neolithic
tendencies toward leisure activities. In
other words, the advent of agriculture gave
birth to boredom, since humans no longer had
to spend all their time working for survival, which gave birth to the culture that
we know of today. In essence, the breadth of
knowledge in the archives of humanity stems

from our ability to manipulate the land and to supply an excess of materials that, consequently, garnished time to wonder. All cultural accessories are a product of boredom. Everything is made for us and jobs are specialized so we get bored on our off-time and thus create and fill the world with accessories that entertain our minds. One could say that culture takes away our synergy with nature whereby, because of our achievements, we exist outside of the natural order of the wild. I think humans will eventually regress toward this synergy as we reach the summit of our gloriousness and everything falls apart.

It was out of such recreation that religion was created. It is interesting to note that the deities and codes of all the religions (monotheistic and pagan) have been a reflection of the culture and environment in which they grew out of. For example, we have the Mesopotamian pagan religion, flourishing before the Greeks, that had a malevolent pantheon.[7] Mesopotamia existed between the Tigris and Euphrates Rivers which made the land fertile for civilization.[8] However, these rivers flooded constantly and unpredictably. In addition, Mesopotamia was positioned in a desert plain with no natural boundaries to keep invaders out, so out of such tension and devastation emerged a culture imbedded with fear.[9] The gods here were fierce, cruel, and demanded respect.

One last example is that of the Old Testament. The god here is, to quote the precision of Richard Dawkins, "arguably the most unpleasant character in all fiction: jealous and proud of it; a petty, unjust, unforgiving control-freak; a vindictive, bloodthirsty, racist, infanticidal, genoci-dal, filicidal, pestilential, megalomanical, sadomasochistic, capriciously malevolent bully."[10] Let's not forget that the Old Testament is patriarchal as well since god is referred to as "The Father". Undoubtedly, the Hebrews who constructed the Old Testament were experiencing ultimate turmoil. As we know from history, the Jews traveled from Canaan (modern-day Israel) in the 17th century BCE to Egypt and became prisoners. They then escaped a couple hun-dred years later via an extensive journey through more desert back to Canaan(scholars debate the exact years in which Moses lead the exodus but some time between the 13th century BCE and 11th century BCE).[11]

Existing in the Middle-East several hundred years after the Hebrews migrated to Egypt was a nascent form of monotheism called Zoroastrianism.[12] A lot of uncer-tainty surrounds the man named Zoroaster, but he is generally thought to have lived about the 6th or 5th century BCE in what was Persia.[13] This philosophy is, in my mind, similar to the Vedic texts of early Hinduism in India but with a slight twist and without the religious structure. Without going into detail just know that basically in Zoroastrianism there is a lifeforce (truth) beneath all things that we need to live in harmony with so we can overcome (untruth). I only mention this because it influenced monotheism into existence.

Whilst in Egypt, the Hebrews experienced a tumultuous political scene with pharaoh dynasties constantly changing laws and engaging in elaborate building projects. The Egyptians had a polytheistic religion, but at one point in the eighteenth dynasty(mid 1300s BCE) the pharaoh Akhenaten decided that only Aten (the disk of the sun) should be worshiped thus starting a early form of monotheism.[14] The Hebrews undoubtedly kept in mind the notion of a primary god when they went back the Middle-East, and it was during the exodus that the Old Testament was polished and secured, with the ideas of Zoroaster and Akhenaten, as the sacred scripture of Judaism.

So jump forward in time a couple thousand years. We now have three monotheistic

religions all influenced by the Old
Testament. We have experienced centuries of
political discord and revampment. We have
experienced the advent of industry and
therefore technology. Our Western culture is
a mosaic of ethnicities and perspectives,
and we are now in what is called the "post-
modern" age. Subjectivity and relativism
permeate all aspects to solve problems of
traditional thought and hopefully find
understanding and equality beneath every-
thing-this paper is an example of postmodernism in ways. Given that I'm writing this
in said time frame many issues still abide
in the world as direct result from traditional thought. I don't necessarily have
answers but as history shows it is the very
act of transmitting ideas that eventually
changes the global mindset. With that said I
will start in on some of my opinions that
correlate with culture.

First of all I want to talk about the
beauty myth and sexism. "The Beauty Myth" is
a sociological concept describing how people
rate their acceptance in society based on
appearance.[15] Research cites media and
religious portrayals, enculturation, legal
barricades, and biological designs and fears
to reveal how looks lead to stratification,
bias, and exploitation.[16] "The Beauty Myth"
mostly relates to females and has such been

qualities we as a human species have to live with difference.

Aside from feminism, I have a few ethical and social thoughts I'd like to share on the topics of family and childbearing. Generation after generation couples decide, after much deliberation, to start a family. Ok, I understand that the human species, like any species, can't continue without procreation, but I find a few ethical concerns about this.

First of all, humans tend to value life to the highest degree and yet we continuously exploit others and engage in violence (this I will discuss in detail in the Purpose Decay section). My question is why bring a life into such a world? I find myself questioning all the time why people have kids in the midst of socio-political tempest. I guess all I can hope for is that this child is brought into an environment with a secure household with plenty of opportunity and benevolence. Humans in this day and age have the tools to gear every child's upbringing toward success. Despite all the rags-to-riches stories, people still need skills and hard work to succeed. The family unit should take the responsibility to teach their children how to survive in the real world. Without a secure household a child may loose advantages further in life

that could've been prevented had certain
precautions been made.

Every once in awhile you hear a teenager claim that "I didn't choose to be born."
This statement used in this setting is full
of naivete and angst and is usually used as
a tool to cop out of responsibility.
However, it is an interesting ethical concern. A name, for example, bequeaths identity and stays with you your whole life(unless
of course the decision is made to change
it), so one could say that they were given
life and a name against their will. In
addition, a name can bear so much weight
based on expectations that identity crises
are established. This all raises questions
about freewill. I mean before one is born
their parents control will, so at what point
does one actually have their own freedom of
will?

It is always entertaining to wonder
about how parents perceive their kid, or
even how others perceive children. The kid
is going to experience the same anatomical
growth as the parents did once puberty
starts and once the child starts school it
will be a long road of socialization, which
is what everyone experiences. Some parents
hold high expectations for their children,
yet it is interesting to think that this bi-
product of sex will inevitably grow up and

potentially hate the parents or make the parents proud. My overall question is why perpetuate the species so willingly without some ethical reflection if randomness of social and neurological elements eventually result in death?

In pre-21st century times(before our current postmodernism) families were had to aid with farming and to expand the community. Since medicine has advanced to were it is, people are born healthier and live longer, yet small cities are hard to come by now and the global population is beyond 6 billion, so what is this mysterious desire that drives the propagation of the species? I call it "The Emotional-Social Intrigue of Nostalgia." I've observed that society gives off various sentiments that make people envious of creating a family. I mean, for example, if a young couple has friends with kids a yearning may develop to experience the fun and mirth of that family. In addition, family albums may play a part in this desire. Looking through family pictures gives off a sense of nostalgia that saddens one into an envious state for creating such memories of their own life.

Another random thought that rattles around in my head from time to time concerns the domestication of animals. I watch people with dogs on leashes, dogs, trained to

bark at trespassers, different breeds of
dogs, dogs sniffing everything, and all the
while humans have to clean up after them and
take care of them. This goes the same for
really any pet but dogs are my best example.
History says that what we nowadays refer to
dogs were domesticated in Eurasia some time
around 15,000 to 100,000 years ago.[28] Also,
it has been noted that dogs ranging from
Chihuahuas to mastiffs all derive from
wolves.[29] In fact, coyotes have more of a
genetic difference than wolves than the
aforementioned dogs.[30] Species in the genus
of Canis, like lupis, latrans, and famil-
iaris, are basically the same species.[31]

Ethical theories abound on the subject
of the treatment of animals, however my
thought is that domesticating animals takes
away their nature. In other words, pets
become extensions of human families and are
trained to behave, yet pets are wild animals
who don't have a culture of rules to understand why not to act a certain way. It may
be fun to have a pet but that pet can't
take of itself if it's been trained to live
through a human. It's like when your told
not to feed the animals in a national park
because the animals will become dependent.
Moreover, the process of domestication isn't
full proof. Pets need to be trained to be
pets via humans.

If your driving down the street and come to a traffic light your likely not to look at the driver sitting in the lane next to you. Why? Because of a phenomenon called cultural norms. Cultural norms are unwritten, practically innate mannerisms that people are conditioned to practice as dictated by the governing cultural framework. It is through media messages and the behaviors of other fellow culturally imbedded individuals that a level of control is transmitted. Cultural norms also play a major role in maintaining the status quo.

In Western culture: women are suppose to have long hair, people are suppose to dress tidy and plain, people aren't suppose to curse all the time, sex isn't suppose to occur in public places, and people like their space. If any of these elements occur in contrast to the norm then a level of discomfort arises. There are a ton of subtle norms in existence and the best way to find them is to do something and wait for disapproval from a public mass. The funny thing about cultural norms is that people just follow the norm and don't question it. I mean so what if society expects a certain image or status quo. One can decide to do whatever one decides to do.

We are drowning in a sea of culture.
All our mores and control structures and
stereotypes infiltrate and impregnate our
minds so much that we don't know what way is
up. These institutions have constructed a
foundation that is indestructible because to
deconstruct it would cause everything to
crumble. This is likened to the game of
Jenga. I refer to it as "The Jenga Effect"
where if any one element of society were
removed society would weaken. Like it or
not, if we don't watch out we will remove
too many pieces and everything will crumble
and implode.

The element preventing "The Jenga
Effect" is what I call "The Temporary Fix
Effect." This effect is really just a redundant, cyclical cover to thwart the
inevitable. Automobiles, for example,
couldn't be built to last forever because
each driver wears the car out differently so
repairs are bound to happen which requires
numerous services to sprout up. The grass
won't stay trimmed, the house won't stay
painted, the grocery stores won't stay
stocked, power plants can't operate by themselves, and products won't make themselves-
enter economics. Economics is about heeding
the many needs of society in order to keep
society going. However, as prices and/or
competition increases quality decreases,

therefore if a product of cheap quality is
purchased it will probably break easily and
create a regeneration of the need that first
purchased it. In other words, businesses
employ people to make goods that will decay,
or be used up, or break so as to continue
the cycle of production, thus temporarily
fixing a problem. The problem is that we
don't know how to break the cycle because
too many elements rely on the cycle. Just
think about all the jobs behind sitting down
at a restaurant and ordering a nice meal.
Managers order the necessary items, ware-
house personnel load and dispatch trucks,
truck drivers deliver the food(this step
opens many jobs on it's own), kitchen staff
then prepare the food, and servers serve it
to you.

    There are many other side affects of
this recoiling of commerce. Society causes
stress by coercing the masses to produce
endlessly that pleasure seeking outlets
form, i.e. smoking, drinking, and entertainment. With the perpetual cycle of commerce
fueled by the coping mechanism of hedonism
society can ultimately be dismantled to
redundancy. I tend to see everything human
around me as repetitious of eons past.
Dialogue has always been the same. People
have always complained about the human condition and people have always had ideas

about change.   Even me writing this paper is
redundant because all the elements I have
incorporated into this work are from the
knowledge archives of the human legacy so
who is to say that my thoughts haven't been
expressed at one point in time or at any
future point.   As humans we think and affect
the world and further the drama by engaging
in cyclical movements.

Aside from redundancy, it is ultimately
the very haphazard interplay of interactions
that has spawned existence. As a thought
experiment try to think about every interaction you have ever made both directly and
indirectly.   Every person who has ever
crossed paths with you has an imprint of you
and probably was changed a tiny bit by your
affect in their microcosm.   Every action
involved in everyone's microcosmic daily
rigor reverberates in a myriad of ways endlessly and has created the macrocosm we all
experience every day.

If each person alter's the world
through their own solipsistic imprints then
to what extent does each person change the
world?

Interestingly, an afterlife could very
well exist purely on the basis of causality.
In other words, during one's life things
were caused and existence was filled with

causing things to be caused and thus being a source of future causality. So every act acted while alive will cause a ripple effect posthumously and thus essentially be as though one lived beyond the grave. Or course one won't be conscious of said after affects of their actions beyond death, but any descendants will still be affected by you based on your actions and genes and life achievements.

To repeat, an uncomprehensible array of imprints exists somewhere in the minds of everyone about everyone they've ever inter-acted with, so every act acts on every other act that is ever acted. The rise of humans toward civilization, culture, and beyond was a result of and is furthered by an endless causal stream of infinite interactions and subsequent interactions all playing on each other all the time. Think before you leap because what you do today may have repercus-sions later. You never know who will be affected and how based on your actions.

---*Of Masks & Masochism*---

"The great majority of mankind are satisfied with appearances, as though they were realities, and are often more influenced by the things that seem than by those that are."-Niccolo Machiavelli

  I often hear people claim events happen for a reason. In fact, it is almost universal to claim this. Reason, however, implies that there is a divine or cosmic purpose for everything. I say that we just think there is a meaning to events, especially if things after the fact turn out better than before. In hindsight everything can be evaluated, and it's the people who have experienced rough times of poverty and desolation that tend to spread their story of overcoming to others. On the other hand, it's worth pondering the infinite amount of counter realities that could have happened had one miniscule element been changed.

  Humans have a propensity to designate meaning in order to make sense of the world as a solipsistic self interpreting the world and trying to cope with the randomness of the infintisimal interactions of all things. In fact, Logotherapy is a school of psycho therapy that focuses specifically on the will to find meaning. Viktor E. Frankl pioneered this form of therapy after surviv-

ing the holocaust. Basically, a psychologist using Logotherapy would work with a
patient to uncover solutions to existential
problems.[1]

It is evident that most horrid events
in history have revamped the world but if
there was a predetermined reason behind all
the occurrences in world history then why
all the blood shed in the first place? Why
all the suffering? And why does human history repeat in cycles and in dialogue? This
ultimate plan, whatever it's eventual apex,
is surely sadistic.

A cause will cause a cause that will
affect an affect exponentially, so what we
classify as a beneficial outcome is a product of a series of previous causes in the
past. Vise versa is true for events that we
label as detrimental. All that can be hoped
for is that your personal trajectory through
time will be filled with mostly the affects
of causes that have had a beneficial course.
Trying to be virtuous to all is an attempt
at ensuring joyful and advantageous outcomes
through the reciprocity of interactions.

Unfortunately, at some point in the
spectrum of time members of this universal
baton race die and this phenomenon is
frightening to us. How do we handle trudging
through time knowing that we die? Why strug-
gle to survive at all costs? Why not just

give up if times get tough or relentless?

The answer is ego. We handle the constant barrage of stimulation to our electrically overactive and complex brains through a sense of self-ness. This mechanism of self-ness makes the body exert its mark on the world in order to feel a sense of control. The underling message of Greek plays, bible fables, and other myths of world religions is how the human ego is detrimental to a peaceful existence with others.

Ego isn't just self-ness(psychologically speaking) its genetic and cultural. This amalgam of sources plays off of other egos resulting in desire, dissent, and expression. Moreover, with a society teeming with time saving devices one can exercise as much free expression as one wants eventually creating more ego clashes. It is from these ego clashes of the world that we are bequeathed a catalogue of arguments of all genres, yet, despite all efforts, it is the human ego that grasps the world we exist in and makes sense of it by reducing confusion to a simple answer.

News flash, there aren't any simple answers. For instance, I maintain that the human path through time is fueled by a pan-behavioral deterministic nurture. In other words, the actions of all things all have biologic phantom controllers that interact

in a world that conditions and teaches and
continuously causes innumerable other causes. I, as you have probably observed by
now, talk about this a lot. The causes of
affects interact with the many psychological
aspects of people living within a society.
Life, can in a way, be viewed as being predetermined because every action puts into
motion every act that is happening and will
happen, so as you live you are experiencing
the effects of causes put into motion in a
previous time. Confusing I know that's why
simple answers are easily understood (i.e.
God willed it). It is simplicity that
soothes our minds into drones. Moreover,
the complexity of emotions and the need to
survive sets the stage for such mechanisms
as hope and meaning.

These defense mechanisms are, elemen-
tarily, masks we use to cope with existence,
ego being the supreme mask. Forgetfulness,
possessions, wealth, religion, clothes, and
motivation are all masks. Masks are everywhere. Constructing masks to help us cope
with the fear of the unknown and the complexities of human life are just another
facet of the human condition.

Interestingly, a trivial glance at the
passing landscapes will suffice for proof.
We plant trees, flowers, and bushes all with
different colors and sizes and we build

artistically magnificent structures to appeal to our wonder all in an attempt to beautify our environment. It's as if humans glorify themselves to mask the true filth of being an animal. Moreover, anything less than human(in our so-called civilized sense) has become taboo, like for instance sex and nudity.

As for the device of hope, we redundantly forget its power yet it nonetheless is a mask. Self-help books, motivational speeches on empowerment, talks about reaching our potentials, optimistic ranks of self worth, and self-esteem building programs are all masks of perseverance.

Even modifying our biologically given images is a mask. We will go through tremendous pain(or claim no pain) in order to get tatoos or piercings just to make ourselves more comfortable with ourselves. What's more, body modification can be anything from a simple piercing to cosmetic surgery to body building.[2]

Essentially, all our masks render us masochists. Those of us that wake up everyday and commute to our temporarily secured future in order to maintain our mundane lives are masochists. Even those homeless beggars on the side of the road that are better off dead are masochists. Furthermore, those single moms who work two minimum wage jobs to support a family in a low income neighborhood are masochists. Those who aren't are the suicidal few who opt not participate in hollow visages and charades any longer.

Ironically, humans in the developed Western world are stressed to such extremes that they render their lives full of suicidal tendencies yet these tendencies just further to mask their strife. Workaholics toil despite obvious self-induced malnutrition and/or sleep deprivation, smokers ingest chemicals that induce cancer, athletes perform aggressively despite obvious bodily breakdowns, and pretty much anyone venturing out into the world has to deal the potential threat of death.

Do you understand what I'm getting at? Anyone who battles against looming desolation obviously enjoys the pain or else they would just give up. Our worldly, ego enhancing facades are a means to prolong our baneful existence. We are masochists hidden behind masks of human made, mind distorting elements in order to survive...

---The Feeble Safeguards of Longevity---

"History shows again and again how nature points out the folly of men."-Blue Oyster Cult[1]

The man versus nature saga is an age old, redundant, and tireless battle of wits between the eternal forces of biology and humanity's conceited yet naive attempt at security. Lest we forget that we are frail and vulnerable to nature's whim. We can try in vain to conquer the Earth's caprices but we ultimately fail. Towns built: on the edges of rivers will flood, on mountains will erode, on the plains will get tornadoes, on beaches will get hurricanes, and in high latitudes will get blizzards. Wind storms ravage trees which subsequently destroy houses. Winter storms restrict the work commute and usually result in car crashes. Even on a microscopic level, nature unleashes bacteria unbeknownst to us which causes much suffering. The irony is that humans love and use nature but we are always caught off guard when nature bites back.

The seven wonders of the ancient world were the Great Pyramids of Giza, the Hanging Gardens of Babylon, the Temple of Artemis at Ephesus, the Statue of Zeus at Olympia, the Mausoleum of Halicarnassus, the Colossus of

Rhodes, and the (Pharos)Lighthouse of
Alexandria.[2] Five out of these seven wonders
are thought to have been destroyed by natural causes, these being: the Statue of Zeus
at Olympia by probable fire[3], the Hanging
Gardens of Babylon having been destroyed by
probable fire[4]; the Mausoleum of
Halicarnassus destroyed possibly by earthquake[5]; the Colossus of Rhodes by
earthquake[6]; and the Lighthouse of
Alexandria by earthquake[7]. It just goes to
show that people can create majestic structures yet nature takes them away. The Temple
of Artemis at Ephesus, however, is thought
to have been destroyed at the hands of men
searching for fame or by invaders.[8]
Luckily, the pyramids still exist yet their
outer white limestone casings are gone.[9]
Even natural wonders mystify us but are cre-
ations of the Earth's forces. The Grand
Canyon in Arizona is a good example being
the product of 6 million years of erosion.[10]

Will we humans ever learn that nature
can't be domesticated? We try and try and
try again to withstand nature's steadfast
fury yet unlucky we have been in surviving.
At times we do succeed, but it's through our
own spontaneous advances in culture and
technology that yield more recoil in the
Earth's destructive power. We invent cars,
medicine, irrigation systems, power plants
and create huge landfills that eventually

but pressure on the Earth's ecology. Gases are emitted into the atmosphere causes a reduction in the ozone which eventually causes ocean levels to rise, deforestation causes the extinction of plants and animals, building cities on fault lines is a recipe for disaster, and so is resorting to town building on or below sea level. I must say, quite misanthropically, that I don't feel sorry for towns that get destroyed by floods or tornadoes or earthquakes because it's our fault for living there.

The Life After People series on the History Channel expresses and showcases hypothetical scenarios dealing with nature's revenge after humans stop their constant control.[11] Plants will take root and destroy buildings when we stop regular grounds maintenance, domestic pets will merge back into the wild (and some breeds of dogs won't survive because the will have lost the ability to swim), damns will break causing immense flooding, famous paintings will fade in sunlight or through bacteria, steel structures will rust when we stop cleaning therefore causing implosion, and eventual fires will erupt due to loss of pressure controls or safeguards in buildings that house beer manufacturing, power sup-plies, fuel reserves, or explosives.

To reiterate, we humans have fabricated a world that self made and we ultimately toil for control to bolster our egos.

Another concept that I have yet to discuss is medicine. We long for a means to prolong our lives which is just as unnatural as paving the roads we have named to effectively transport ourselves. In this post-industrial information age we have cured diseases that once wiped away millions in times of yore. In addition, we are constantly researching ways to eliminate even more ills. Smallpox is gone, polio is gone, measles is gone, cancers of all kinds are slowly being rectified, we have vaccines for influenza, we have countless pills and therapies from everything from arthritis to colds to parkinson's disease, we have Braille for the blind, prosthetics for amputees, glasses for people who are loosing vision, and transplant technology. We even market hand sanitizers and disinfectants to keep at a moments reach to thwart any germs.

Are we becoming to clean and healthy for our own good? If we want to cure all diseases and prolong lifespans we will need to cure absolutely everything and govern all exposure to any possible virus because if not any mutant strain will kill us off due to our supreme cleanliness. What's more, if we prepared ourselves for every possible future malady we wouldn't get anything done or do anything life expanding because we would be afraid of hurting ourselves or getting sick. A line has to be drawn. Do we go through life getting sick and getting hurt so our bodies build immunity and endurance or do we lock ourselves up behind science?

Throughout this book human ego is investigated along with the many conflicting elements of humanity, but the man versus nature dilemma is just as concerning. Nature is the silent enemy. Nature has always lurked in the shadows of humanity's strife. Unfortunately, the natural underpinnings of the cosmos have the upper hand in history. We either have to control everything and fulfill anthropocentric destiny or learn synergy. One thing is for sure, nature will get revenge, and someday the Earth won't be able to house us. We have a lot of troubles at hand that are increasing our need to find ways to live beyond the Earth. All things considered, humans have to come together and concentrate all energy on space research and environmental regeneration before nature erases us.

- - - The Cauldron of Scientific Entities - - -

"Countless dark bodies are to be inferred beside the sun-and we shall never see them. Among ourselves this is a parable; and a psychologist of morals reads the whole writing of the stars only as a parable-and sign language which can be used to bury much in silence."-Friedrich Nietzsche (Beyond Good and Evil)

I have two words for you-time and beauty. Or rather cosmology and biology. Two subjects I want to explore in this section are how time has existed long before humans ever existed and will exist far beyond our legacy and how beauty is only skin deep and how science has revealed so much about our bodies. Reader be warned this chapter contains some mind-boggling statistics and grotesque opinions about human nature.

First I will tackle time and space. Scientists exploring space have revealed that a galaxy has 100 billion stars and there are 100 billion galaxies in the universe.[1] [2] That stat alone is enough to point out how infintisimal human lives are in the cosmos. If we aren't alone in the universe we sure are extremely lonely.

To refresh your memory, a light year is the distance light travels in a year-which is equivalent to 186,282 miles per second[3], so for light to be traveling that fast from its source it could take eons to reach us if it was incredibly far away. What's more, some of those stars may not even exist anymore because the light is just now reaching us. If such stars were supernovas and imploded millions of years ago we are basically viewing the past as we look into the sky.[4] [5] Eventually, as studies in cosmology reveal, our known constellations will soon dissipate due to time catching up with light travel.[6] [7]

Cosmologists estimate that the diameter of a typical galaxy is tens of thousands of light-years across[8] [9], and the typical distance between two neighboring galaxies is only a few million light-years.[10] [11] In addition, the universe is 13.6 billion years old.[12] [13] Some researchers hold that the universe will expand so much that matter will be destroyed-thus named the Big Rip or Big Crunch.[14] [15] This is a closed universe theory that goes on to suggest that if there is enough matter for the expansion of the universe to be halted and then reversed the universe would collapse, subsequently resulting in future Big Bangs.[16] [17]

As the universe slowly expands and ages and the light from distant explosions ceases then the night sky will be darker. If humans manage to inhabit Earth(or any surrounding planet) that long to view the Big Rip(which is unlikely because the sun will have become a red giant in 5 billion years and engulf and destroy the orbits of the inner planets including Earth)[18] [19] then extensive evolution has occurred and the social environment has changed so much and extended far beyond our current comprehension that anything existing nowadays will seem like it never existed.

Chemists working with cosmologists and physicists also have discovered how and where the elements of the periodic table are created. Interestingly, every element heavier(having more protons and neutrons) were formed from supernova explosions far off in space.[20] Deep in the cores of stars is enough heat to cause nuclear fusion and thus form new elements-this process is called stellar nucleosynthesis.[21] From this the elements from atomic numbers 6(carbon) to at least 94(plutonium) have been created naturally.[22] All others on the periodic table are man made.[23] This all means that the vast majority of the compounds that make up everything around us have been elsewhere in the universe at some point in time.

Ultimately, the very materials that we and our possessions our made out of (as I briefly mentioned in "Created Concepts") is actually space dust that traveled via stellar wind and meteor showers until billions of years later were joined together with other compounds to create life and it's accessories. Just think, all the atoms(except probably hydrogen) have been recycled throughout the history of the universe and will continue to be recycled.

Despite altering views on the superfluous and metaphysical, once we die we never exist again as our current form because of this migration of atoms. One could reason that, in essence, the atoms that make us up are eternal, therefore past lives are a result of various atoms from previous forms of life whereas the after life is an unknown destination for traveling atoms.

Its astounding that humans aggrandize themselves when in fact their existence on this huge rock cluster has only been an inkling of time. It's safe to say that the universe is overwhelmingly large, old, and increasingly unknown and yet humans are spoiled and can't comprehend their own triviality. My point to all this rabbling is that, to quote the song Shroud of False by Anathema, "We are just a moment in time. A blink of an eye. A dream for the blind."[24]

My personal koan for the thoughts rendered by these scientific findings is that:

time will extend far beyond our misery and anxiety. A repetition of that seems to quell any drama I may experience. It may be considered passive and life-negating (i.e. nihilistic) to just let go and be content, but, in sum, no one will escape time nor its materialistic, chaotic powers of regeneration and transformation.

Looking at the opposite sex, especially while aroused, will probably render several feelings of attraction. Take, for example, a man engaging in small talk with a female co-worker who happens to be gorgeous and he is secretly becoming aroused. Before continuing I have to clarify some underlying facts. First off, the male (and most likely society) thinks this female is gorgeous because she fits the social standard of beauty-tall, slender, long hair, noticeable cup size, makeup, and high heels. All these characteristics fall under the category of the beauty myth (see The Tempest Sea of Culture for further explanation). So in reality this guy is really just turned on due to enculturation. In addition, as humans get aroused the hypothalamus in the brain releases sex hormones that stimulate the reproductive organs.[25] So this guy is basically indoctrinated by society's sex images and controlled neurally by chemicals.

Moreover, one must keep in mind that a woman's curves are such due to biology's design to aid in child birth. For instance, a woman's pelvis is tilted to form a bowl for a fetus to grow, a woman's hips are wide to allow stability while pregnant, adipose tissue settles more around the hips of a female thus creating large buttocks and thighs(whereas on a man adipose tissue generally settles in the belly hence "beer belly"), and a woman's back is arched also for stability.[26] Furthermore, mammary glands (boobs) are modified sweat glands that produce milk.[27] So ultimately the guy in my example is becoming aroused involuntarily but can't see his err. One, the female didn't decide to be female; two, the beauty myth is so culturally embedded that either gender can't control the craving to live up to social standards; three, both genders are made of the same material and experience the same world therefore have more in common than one might think; and four, each culture has different views on what is beautiful and what implies fertility.

In this culture we play the dating game whereas some cultures have pre-ordained marriages. Psychologists study this game and the affects of sex appeal to better understand this phenomenon. People tend to always seek the most attractive person not matter how attractive they might be.[28] Moreover, people generally end up partnering up with people who rank at roughly the same attractiveness level.[29] Biologically, the look of fertility warrants mating so that genes will have a better chance of survival.[30] In our culture, however, more comes to the table than just looks. Wealth, security, possessions, and reliability are most of the characteristics that people look for in a date or potential date.[31]

Also, on the opposite, this game can get ugly. On this side of the spectrum, it's the lecherous fiends that enjoy this game in hopes of "playing the field" for sexual conquests. These types might also just be out to manipulate and take advantage of other's loneliness. Ultimately, dating is a complex stage of wits with unpredictable outcomes but people will still play because no one really knows what they want.

I must digress for a bit and disclose some rather disturbing thoughts that are rather obvious but need pointing out. First, we all came from the coupling of an ovum and a sperm.[32] Second, we all grew in a females' uterus until birth.[33] Three, we all came out of a vagina(unless via Ceasarian). Four, we all defecated and urinated ourselves during infancy. And, finally, five, we all still engage in the discharge of waste only now more discreetly. I've found that knowing such information about sex and bodily functions has caused in me nihilistic disdain for sexuality. I mean it's a complete turn off to think of someone who is attractive sitting on/standing over the toilet disposing of waste material. Moreover, a female is a female and a male a male. There is no other option. It's boring and redundant to habitually be attracted to that which every member of the respective gender has.

There is a plethora of other information regarding the body that I should also mention at this time. I think it best to use another thought experiment to describe these upcoming science facts. Either stand in front of a mirror or just look down at your body(it doesn't matter what gender you are) and think about what's under your skin. Remember the common saying that beauty is skin deep? Well we are leaving the realm of outside appearances and superficiality and revealing the complex labyrinth of complex biological systems. Ok, so looking at your body you see hairs all over and in numerous parts. Hair is basically biomaterial composed mostly of the protein keratin.[34] Hair growth begins inside the hair follicle.[35] The only "living" portion of the hair is found in the follicle.[36] The hair that is

visible is the hair shaft, which exhibits no
biochemical activity and is considered
"dead".[37] Dead cells accumulate at the base
of the follicle and are cornified-mixed with
keratin.[38] Sorry to dissapoint but hair is
just dead cells, which happen to insulate
the body. Hair is also vestigial in humans.
Hair at one point served as fur and greatly
insulated our bodies but as time progressed
and different DNAs mixed and environments
changed humans ceased to need as much hair.
We have clothes now to serve what hair used
to.

At further glance, our skin is colored.
Melanin is what gives skin it's hue. Melanin
is a cell type that protects from UV
light.39 Based on what environment your
lineage stemmed from will most likely determine your melanin quantities. For instance,
a white person has less melanin due to the
limited sun light that generally occurs in
European countries, and black people have
more melanin due to high amounts of sun
exposure most likely resulting from desert-
like environments.[40]

Another visual of the underworld is
blood vessels. Each square inch of human
skin consists of twenty feet of blood vessels.[41] In other words, there are 60,000
miles of blood vessels in the body, and 10
billion capillaries.[42] In addition: there

are 206 bones in adults with the strength
enough to support 20 times the body's
weight; 650 muscles; 45 miles of nerves;
about 100 trillion cells in the body; a com-
pound of chemicals worth about $20; we sali-
vate a pint everyday to aid with eating; we
shed about 600,000 particles of skin every
hour; each day we inhale and exhale nearly
20,000 breaths; an adult has about 30 billion fat cells; and inside each little bump
on the top and sides of your tongue are 200
or more taste buds, and they reproduce themselves every week or two if damaged.[43] Most
intriguing is that about 98.4% of our genetic code match those of chimps, and 99.9%
match those of other humans.[44] What's more,
our 1.6% difference from chimps has enabled
space travel, and the 0.1% person-to-person
variation results in differences in individual traits.[45]

In summation, there is a cauldron of
scientific information at our disposal and
it's bubbling over. What are we going to
make out of this brew? Shall we treat people
with respect knowing that the very elements
of our bodies are similar whereas it's just
our egotistical cultural and traditional
ties that yield dissent? Are we to use our
knowledge to cure diseases and make humanity
more benevolent as a whole? Are we to calm

ourselves in the face of time? Are we to
sublimate sexual desires in favor of intelligence and self-protection? Most importantly we have to ask ourselves what kind of
creature are we to become when we realize
the synergistic matrix of all things. The
ashes of human ego should be like the water
evaporating from this pot of boiling knowledge...

Purpose
Decay
- - - *Teleologically Thwarted Legacy* - - -

"Not to honor men of worth will keep the people from contention; not to value goods which are hard to come by will keep them from theft; not to display what is desirable will keep them from being unsettled of mind."
-Lao-Tzu(Tao te Ching)

Humans have always claimed superiority on this planet yet, despite of all our successes, we still act foolish and begrudging to others. There exists what I call "The Ultimate Paradox" between intelligence and lack there of amongst humans. People are driven by self-preservation to such an extreme that they will exploit others to get ahead. It's ironic to me that humans place such high value on life despite their general disregard and disrespect for their fellow beings.

How you may ask has such a paradox spawned? Well as I see it Western culture has an "Individualist Paradigm" that encourages self-reliance and uniqueness. All the inventions, ideologies, and pleasures in the world are a direct result from this constant desire to be original and stand out. It is this very paradigm that is the cause of this paradox. Stand back and think for a second. Everyone is out for themselves because society puts so much pressure on success, and everyone has possessions and families to protect, and everyone is thinking about their own futures, so, ultimately, everyone will do whatever it takes to survive to fulfill social expectations regardless of what the consequences are.

In other words take this example, cigarette companies knowingly sell products that cause ill-health and cause bad habits but they aren't concerned with anything but money. Furthermore, these companies employ people who need money to survive, so people who work for these companies don't care about the thousands of people who die every year from the product so long as they get paid. That's a concern for the whole world. People are happy for any job, but it's the countless marketers and CEOs that are profiting the most.

It is this work-to-survive conundrum that can't be broken and every aspect of commerce knows this. This quagmire exactly defines social Darwinism. Companies will use any trick they can to stay alive and the workers of the world don't argue as long as they get to stay alive too.

This "Individualist Paradigm" also requires one to multi-task in order to maximize efficiency in the workplace. Everyone wants to get a ton done all at the same time to maximize efficiency. Companies encourage it because the more one person can do the less need for more employees. Moreover, the faster products or services can be dished out the faster money can be made by allowing room for more customers. George Ritzer gave this behavior the moniker of "McDonaldization." Ritzer defines "McDonaldization" as "the process by which the principles of the fast-food restaurants are coming to dominate more and more sectors of American society as well as the rest of the world."[1] The idea behind the assembly line is being incorporated into all aspects of industry. Everyone seems to have so much to do and no patience to wait that the faster one can eat, exercise, buy, learn, and fix stuff the more time there is for more activity. Unfortunately, this fast paced world induces massive amounts of stress.

The pressure to multi-task comes at a price. If we push ourselves too hard our body gets tired and then our immune systems

weaken and the next thing we know we have a
baneful illness. Stress diverts energy from
the disease fighting system rendering us
more likely to get sick.[2] It is also noted
that wounds heal slower in stressful environments.[3] What's more, those who react
with anger over little things are the most
prone to coronary heart disease.[4] The fats
released during stress linger in the blood-
stream and help form plaque that clogs
arteries.[5] While making blood available to
the extremities, stress also constricts
blood vessels in the heart decreasing blood
flow.[6] Negative emotions may also contribute
to poor health practices.
Psychophysiological illnesses (a.k.a. psy-
chosomatic illnesses to laypeople; however
professionals tend to use the term psychophysiological to better describe these
situations) are another stress related element that arises from chemical imbalances
that recoil after stressful situations.[7]
These are when people actually make themselves sick via stress.

I met a friend at a bar once and I
wondered why so many people would frequent a
bar and pay double for drinks when the economy is so bad. He told me, quite candid,
that "What else would you do if your life
sucked?" It got me thinking. People would
rather take the edge off at a noisy bar with

strangers in the hopes of finding sex or getting drunk than staying home safe and sound. It seems like drinking, smoking, engaging in sex, and or any other potential- ly self destructive behavior is an outlet for stress, but in reality those activities may cause greater stress over time.

There is another famous outlet for stress in our society that is ubiquitous, expedites information, and otherwise satis- fies our craving for leisure and that's tel- evision. TV is entertaining and educational but it also has the power to corrupt. On one station you will see a millionaire athlete play a simple sport, on the next you'll see a news story about death and violence, you'll watch hilarious standup comics, a reality show about trying to be a superstar, then another reality show about the life of a superstar. Yet there are also channels that explore or reveal the history behind real events, or there will even be documen- taries on scientific discoveries. However, the general populace tends to watch televi- sion to vegetate and subdue themselves. What's more, impressionable people, such a kids and quite possibly the fantasy prone types, yearn to have what they see or do what they see as their brains are infiltrat- ed by the media via television.

Most television programs(and movies) reflect the socio-political environment of the times. For example, the Godzilla, mutant plants, the nuclear-family and space travel movies and shows of the 1950s and 1960s reflected Cold War terrors and post WW11 ideals.[8] Technophobia is a genre of film which expresses the fears of new and unknown sciences.[9] Movies about giant mutants and creatures of radiation were made in response to nuclear testing.[10] In addition, more recent films also use technophobia to reflect advancements in technology.[11] All in all, media programs mirror ideologies and experiences of the times.

If Godzilla et al. were a cultural reflection of the Cold War Era then what role do television shows of the new millennium suggest about the recent couple of decades?

As I mentioned briefly in "Created Concepts", we are experiencing a social trend of fear. Fear of economic disaster, fear of third-world uprisings, and fear of too much subjectivity. No one religion is correct anymore, no one power system has power, everyone in the world wants to be rich and live the American Dream, and everyone is pressured to work harder, produce more for little, and pay bills with less money. People and society have a lot to

loose so fear of insecurity becomes a great
issue. We are making ourselves panophobic.
We read or hear about death everywhere and
thus become afraid to fly or drive. And we
learn about sickness at a fast food restaurant so we don't go out. Fear perpetuates
avoidance and do we really need people
avoiding things that help the economy just
because the media reports a horror? And do
we want fear mongering passed to further
generations?

I think the entertainment of today sat-
isfies the very same worries as it always
has. One can turn the tv on and live vic-
ariously through supermodels, rich athletes,
rock stars, magicians, etc. Superheroes, via
tv, are still as popular as they were when
they first came out decades ago, so I think
people obsess over these icons because they
yearn to be super themselves. Heck why not?
If people had super powers they could be
more productive, or so that they could get
more social attention and vanquish their low
self esteem and lower-class desperation.
Even ancient societies had stories of
heroes. Since human history is so saturated
with these visions of grandiose maybe we
secretely want our egos to be bigger out of
fear of our mortality?

This "Ultimate Paradox" I speak of is

fueled by the indoctrination of individualism from an early age. Its unfortunate that
one can't grasp the breadth of universal
community at such an age. Religion has
tried but the nascent brain of a child needs
structure, discipline, and answers before it
can fully grasp an others oriented existence. It is also due to the under developed brain that children can't really understand the concept of God, so why impregnate
and corrupt their minds with beliefs that
are beyond their scope. This reaffirms my
point about restructuring familial traditions. Austerity toward a certain perspective about the world is like brand loyalty
only for cultural and religious bias. We
should instill the facts about hedonism
early on instead of masking them with religion. With as archaic as religion is it is
too dull and powerless to the rapidly
increasing cunning of new generations and
cultural change. We need a new weapon. And
we need to start a program for the future
quickly.

Psychological and geographical research
has found that the age of colonization was
due to individualism based and an individual
exertions to stray from the herd and try new
things.[12] No wonder that modern world colonization was led not by Asians, who are
reluctant to cut social and family ties

(collectivism), but by the the more individualistic Europeans.[13] And no wonder that
countries colonized by Europeans willing to
leave family and friends are today highly
individualistic.[14] This quest is over and
also should be this austere notion of individualism. Don't get me wrong, uniqueness
in character has spawned all the inventions
and ideas in the world. Rather we need a
balance of individualism and collectivism.

In fact, research finds that individualism can come at the cost of more loneliness, more divorce, more homicide, and more
stress-related disease.[15] Individualists
also demand more romance and personal fulfillment in marriage, which subjects the
marriage relationship to more pressure.[16] It
has also been noted that meaningless stems
from individualist cultures because there is
a detachment to something greater.[17] Sure
religion has "God" to glue people together,
but religion is too deep rooted and person-
alized in the mind's of people's traditions
to allow a secular human community to exist.
It is ironic that religions preach peace and
community but the belief structures ultimately clash with the idea of secularism,
which is about universal understanding.

What I'm basically saying it that the
"Individualist Paradigm" need be revamped
and aimed for collectivism because humanity

has reached a point were the pressures of population and the need to be independent and arrogant, due to cultural affinities, will cause a downfall and thwart our ability to render a global community of humans.

Let me ask this, why do we send our children to school for over a decade? Is it in hopes of creating a better world or does schooling aid in more sophisticated predator behavior? If schooling is to teach children to become human then the word "human" has more weight than biological. In other words, enculturation(or rather self-domestication) is aimed at making our offspring privy to something more than a mere animal. What defines a human in our minds is not just that we are bipedal and have larger brains but rather we have culture and civilization. Schooling is a means to socialize growing humans into a valuable resource for world commerce. It's almost as if humans are trained to be drones of utility to further the monetary noise and lavish mental accessorizing of the world. And this leads to my paradox about what our ultimate aim really is.

The smoking gun here is our inability to control our pleasure seeking brains, and ultimately human error which includes hostility toward anything that threatens our cherished individual schemas and programs.

Speaking only from the generation in which I grew up I can only reflect on the behavior of my peers thus I have to say that sex is quite omnipresent and freely expressed and therefore the driving force in human error producing behavior. Sexual innuendoes, for example, infiltrate the media, clothing trends advocate the showing of more skin than generations of yore, and, due to natural proclivities, the display of sex reacts with the innate hormonal shift in teenagers and results in high schools teeming with promiscuity. Everyone becomes confused on these matters when on the one hand sex is bad and on the other sex is fun and great. With a gradual introduction of other hedonist behavior we get a culture seething with moral battles. Moreover, we get a lost sense of worldliness.

Only a glimpse at a tabloid magazine or a beer commercial or a blockbuster movie will suffice as evidence that sex sells. Sex is becoming less and less taboo, yet is still demonized by religion. As a matter of fact sex is power. In addition, the marketing of love and sex is big business. Online dating, cosmetics, aesthetics, dieting, pornography, clothing, and pretty much anything that promotes anything through use of family values or carnal pleasure is used against people to spend money. Just think,

sex for procreation yields more family members to perpetuate family traditions and
prejudices, the beauty myth controls and
manipulates people into standards of sex
appeal thus perpetuating a lucrative market,
loneliness and desperation open the door for
pornography, tales abound about nubile maid-
ens that have been fought over, and ancient
cultures held ideals of fertility.

Albeit a new age of physical freedom
and personal discovery I tend to agree with
religious notions of sublimation. With our
technological age and population expediting
there is more at stake if one's reputation
is ruined by sexual desire. We can loose
our job because the boss finds pornography,
previous lovers can black-mail us, the law
can finds us guilty of pedophilia, divorce
takes all our will and money, our date
exploits us and ruins us financially, or
society shuns us for an alternative
lifestyle.

My original idea behind purpose decay
was how the enviousness and wonder of sex
lead to unhealthy and unintellectual
thoughts. My idea was in fact influenced by
the Taoist quote at the beginning of this
chapter. As innate as sex is, and the
desire thereof, it doesn't coincide with
intelligence and intellectual behavior. If
sexual images didn't permeate the world then

I think sexual oriented issues like harass-
ment and discrimination would decrease.
Moreover, if there wasn't a war on sex there
wouldn't be mass hysteria over it's morality. Sex is real but needs to be contained
modestly for the enrichment of intelligent
inquiry and the legacy of humankind. We have
the mental power to sublimate our desires.

Two aspects that have lead me to my
radical thoughts are the teenage delinquency
and the cruel dating games of today's world.
First of all, teens would rather waste their
youth smoking, drinking, playing video
games, watching television, and fornicating
than exploiting their brain's plasticity.
The teenage environment, especially in
Western culture, includes so much peer pressure to conform or rebel that scholarly
pious or intellectual investigation is
pushed aside.

The second facet of the human condition, and a tortuous one at that, is dating.
It all starts in wonder and weeks later ends
in disaster. I find myself questioning why
one would engage in such a matter without
careful consideration of one's own personal
desires. True love is advertised as a timeless, magical experience but in reality people go from date to date in rapid succession
with blind folds on. I think that the people who do find their so-called true love

have succumbed to the world's trick to perpetuate the world and keep money flowing. Is
there such thing as a soulmate? Sure, a
friendship can become so close as to render
a special bond, but in terms of lovers the
spectrum is really undefinable and is an
abyss of complications. I feel that people
these days don't spend enough time knowing
themselves before being washed away by the
sea of pleasures so often bombarded by our
peer groups and the media. Our culture
thrives off self confusion which in turn
creates a market for everything from religion to sex. And even the issue of homosexu-
ality is feared. As far as I am concerned
intimate love is just a mutual campanionship
so who cares if it is between the same gender. There's people who never find campanionship. I personally don't care what sexual appetites people have as long as my comfort isn't encroached. All in all, humans
are weird so deal with it.
     That Taoist quote, however, doesn't
necessarily pertain directly to just the
display of sexually desirous objects but
rather to any desirous object. People suc-
cumb to their desires too willingly and a
snowball effect occurs wherein people loose
track of their finances and modesty. In
addition, that quote deals with issues of
megalomania in people who hold positions of

power and with being flamboyant with posse-
sions that others don't have.

In sum, we humans have cognizance and
such cognizance has changed the world thus
far yet we still need to use our innate powers to make us better than the mere animals
we behave like. In other words, have we
forgotten our purpose to ever expand and
advance our intellect? To increasingly discover and scour the cosmos for new information that will enhance our species and our
progeny? To bring about peace on Earth by
setting aside all our indifferences? To
ultimately exist as a humanitarian creature
exalting a virtuous character? Have we forgotten or misplaced this dream in favor of
the barrage of pleasures and notions exposed
to our psyches? If we can endlessly create
devices that make our existence easier(and
thus make us lazier) than why can't we eliminate evil in the world? And why in the face
of all our worldly knowledge do we choose to
engage in self-destructive behavior? And why
is it that us humans exert so much time
manipulating others for self or group gain?
Just think, if we transferred all the energy
we use to fight, hate, and manipulate people
we'd probably have cured cancer by now or
better.

---*Dissonant Moral Architecture*---

" Nothing is at last sacred but the integrity of our own mind"- Ralph Waldo Emerson

" The truths of religion are never so well understood as by those who have lost the power of reasoning" - Voltaire

Look at the many religions of the world. All claim to have truth, and all disagree with one another. The monotheistic religions all claim their god is in control. A couple other belief systems, like Buddhism and Taoism, have no god but rather seek a self attaining enlightenment wherein the self is in control. Why do humans fight over religions that all preach togetherness and the fundamentals of the human condition? Is the Christian bible any more correct that the Muslim Qur'an? If all sacred scriptures were written by people expressing spiritual feelings about a phantom creator or about metaphysics then all religious thought is an extension of imaginative boredom via story-telling. This coincides with what I mentioned in "The Tempest Sea of Culture" about how all philosophical thought(or rather any complex thought that generates an opinion of the world) is atavistic of Neolithic tendencies toward leisure activities. Moving on, dogma after dogma proposes kindness albeit some direct their kindness just to fellow worshippers while others focus on kindness to all things. Why do so many religions differ and why do people take their scripture literally and coerce others through fear and punishment to convert? Some more than others might have better teachings but should there be a synergy of religiosity for the progression of humanity? How does limiting or manipulating knowledge fulfill compassionate dogma? How does destroying archives of knowledge help evolve humanity's quest for ultimate intelligence and mastery of the universe?

In this section I will explore these questions along with the grotesque behavior of religious fanaticism, the breadth and synthesis of world religions, and finally some general tidbits on the subject from my own philosophical perspective that correspond to my thesis.

Christianity holds the first prize trophy for fanaticism. Aside from the monstrous array of mind manipulating marketing tactics of present-day Evangelists, the single most atrocious example of gullibility by early Christians is believing in "indulgences".

Christian hierarchy during the Middle Ages, got into the habit of selling "indulgences" or tickets into heaven that absolved sin only through morality.[1] Money raised by these indulgences were used for many right-eous causes, both religious and civil, such as building churches, universities, and bridges.[2] In current Roman Catholic doc-trine, one can only receive an indulgences if they have no unabsolved mortal sin.[3] However, one pope, during the Renaissance, exploited this commodity when faced with The Protestant Reformation, starting with Martin Luther's 95 Theses in 1517.[4]

Giovanni di Lorenzo de' Medici (Pope Leo X) came from a powerful family In Italy that spanned many generations and fueled the Renaissance, so Giovanni aspired to further that legacy by using any means necessary.[5] Pope Leo's main idea behind selling "indul-gences" was the hope to keep the Reformation subdued by offering more opportunities for salvation to Catholics.[6] To make matters worse, Leo's papacy held opulent parties known for serving rare delicacies such as peacock' tongues.[7] In addition, jokes and jesters were never hard to find parading about.[8] Leo's natural liberality, his polit-ical ambitions, and his immoderate personal luxury, exhausted within two years the hard savings of Julius II(the previous pope), and precipitated a financial crisis.[9] He did however try to develop and improve Rome. Unfortunately, Leo's decision to sell "indulgences" just seemed like a panacea to aid in economic downfall. Furthermore, Pope Leo also sold cardinals' hats.[10] Now does deceiving the faithful out of money for papal enjoyment, papal irresponsibility, and absolution of sins sound ethical?

Next on my list of intelligence-thwarting religious behavior is the art and habit of book burning. The early Christians so arrogantly elevated their doctrine above all others and refused to let any of their congregation to think in any other way that they concocted a list a banned literature. The Index Librorum Prohibitorum ("List of Prohibited Books") was a list of publications prohibited by the Catholic Church. This list was established in 1557 by Pope Paul IV and continued until 1966, when Cardinal Alfredo Ottaviani declared that there would be no more editions.[11] The avowed aim of the list was to protect the faith and morals of the faithful by preventing the reading of immoral books or works containing theological errors. Books thought to contain such errors included some scientific works by leading astronomers such as Johannes Kepler's Epitome Astronomiae

Copernicianae, which was on the Index from 1621 to 1835.[12] The various editions of the Index also contained the rules of the Church relating to the reading, selling and pre-emptive censorship of books, including translations of the Bible into the "common tongues".[13] The Index included a number of authors and intellectuals whose works are widely read today in most leading universities and are now considered as the foundations of science.

It has also been inferred that the Dark Ages were a direct result from the banning of scientific and philosophical inquiry. Ignorance of how diseases spread from port to port and animal to animal was the leading cause of the plague,[14] but since science contradicted dogma no one knew how to successfully stop it until 1894.[15] The next thing Europe knows twenty-five million people were dead.[16] The jury is still out but the lack of knowledge seems like a possible smoking gun.

Even in the midst of today's melting-pot, subjective culture we still face public outcry over books that unintentionally challenge religious thought. One example is the uproar over the <u>Harry Potter</u> series. Religious debates over this series of books by J. K. Rowling stem largely from assertions that the novels contain occult or

Satanic subtexts.[17] The American Library
Association defines a "challenge" to a book
as any attempt to "remove or restrict materials, based upon the objections of a person
or group."[18] Harry Potter books topped the
list of most challenged books for four years
in a row: 1999, 2000, 2001, and 2002.[19]
Most libraries and schools have instituted
"opt-out" policies which allow parents to
exclude their children from being exposed to
material they object to.[20] A lot of the
uproar has occasionally led to widely publi-
cized legal challenges, often on the grounds
that witchcraft is a government-recognized
religion and that to allow the books to be
held in public schools violates the separation of church and state.[21] Book burnings
have even occurred based a religious fervor.
It's ironic to me that one would criticize
fiction when religious scripture corrupts
all the same. Has traditional thought snow-
balled to the point where any slightly popular cultural trend is seen as a threat?
Can't children just enjoy reading something
fun without some organization banning it
because it's popular?

Controlling the distribution of books
and/ or burning libraries is an excellent
tactic to prevent rebellion or questioning
but is it just? Furthermore, is this tactic

something that has hindered humanistic evolution?

Continuing along these lines, the
Catholic Church also used subliminal messages in the arts to mold thought. During
Early Christian an Byzantine eras in art
history, immense planning went into despoil-
ing the intellect of devotees by establish-
ing a monopoly of symbols. For instance,
the construction of churches, paintings, and
sculptures dematerialize and stylize images
that in turn invite spirituality and unfortunately fear.

Eleventh century Byzantine artists,
for example, eliminated narrative in their
paintings and mosaics in an attempt to
direct more attention to the scene.[22] It was
thought that the viewer had no choice but to
focus on the religious image of the piece
while not being distracted by various other
secular images.

Whereas Byzantine art existed primarily
in Eastern Europe, the western side of
Europe was experiencing a Romanesque style
of art and out of that grew the architectur-
al style known as the Gothic style emerging
in the 1200s.[23] Gothic art is usually associated with stained glass windows and large,
ominous cathedrals that flourished mostly in
France. Art of this era has been character-
ized by a lack of classical structure(the

term "gothic" is a moniker later defined by art historians to classify art that existed after the barbaric Goths from the north invaded and ruined Roman culture).[24]

Gothic cathedrals, as a matter of fact, took the subliminal messaging tactic of Byzantine art to new levels. For starters, most gothic cathedrals(and earlier churches) are designed to represent the iconic image of the cross. This was called the Latin-cross plan: long nave and short transept in the middle region.[25] Furthermore, religious scholars through the ages have viewed Gothic cathedrals as the literal House of God because the immense size and the distribution of light that passes through the windows elevating spiritual thought.[26]

Christianity above all else used what is called "syncretism" in their art and religious foundations in order to acquire converts and keep them. This tool alone secured Christianity's place in Europe and paved the way for its eventual rise to the top of the religious hierarchy.

To start, many commonly worshiped symbols of Christians actually stem from older and previous religions. The fish symbol, for example, has become mostly associated with Jesus and his miracle of feeding 5000[27], yet the fish has many meaning spanning many cultures. Priests of the cult of

Ea, the Mesopotamian god of the waters and
of wisdom, also attached sacred meaning to
the fish.[28] Moreover, Hindus view fish as
avatars of Vishnu and Varuna due to bound-
less liberty and resilience to the Flood.[29]
Even the Buddha had fish on the soles on his
feet which symbolized freedom from worldly
desires.[30] Fish have also been associated
with sexuality due to their fast propagation.[31] Lastly, in China fish are emblems
of plenty and good luck.[32]

Moving on, the symbols of the Four
Evangelists also transcend Christian fundamentalism. Mark the lion, Matthew the
winged-man, Luke the ox, and John the eagle
can symbolize many things. It is also noted
that these motifs originate from the "Old
Testament". Specifically the Book of Ezekiel
in the Book of Revelation. Ezekiel envi-
sioned these four "living creatures" draw
the throne-chariot of God, the Merkabah, and
thus became associated with the Four
Evangelists later in history.[33] However,
the four images also represent the four
fixed signs of the zodiac- the Ox(bull),
representing the sign of Taurus, the lion
the sign of Leo, the Eagle of the sign of
Scorpio, and the man, symbol of the sign of
Aquarius.[34] Christians on the other like to
disassociate their icons away from any pagan
reference and thus say that Mark represents

Christ as king(lions are like kings of animals and because lions were believed to
sleep with open eyes, a comparison with
Christ in the tomb), Matthew represents
Christ's human nature, Luke represents not
only the sacrifice of Christ but that of
followers, and John represents the joining
with Heaven and Christ's ascension.[35]

The cross itself even holds meaning in
various religious arenas besides
Christianity. For instance, the four points
created by a cross represented the four
phases of the moon for the Babylons and the
four great gods of the elements for the
Syrians.[36] A cross within a square symbolized the earth and stability for the
Chinese.[37] Furthermore, the Egyptians had
the ankh that symbolized immortality which
was incorporated into Christianity by the
Coptic Church.[38]

Aside from just the basic symbolism,
Christianity's triumph was assured, not by
divine agency but by three key factors: the
broad base of its appeal to those searching
for what was lacking in Rome's state religion; its acceptance of all people of whatever social station, race, or gender; and
its belief that the kingdom of god was at
hand.[39] All of christianity's rivals had
intentional or advertent barriers to membership: jews had to be circumcised, slaves and

women couldn't worship Mithra, and there were initiations that granted membership into pagan religions.[40] Christianity welcomed anybody. Moreover, Christians had a world view of all things leading inevitably to the culmination of a divine plan. Thus, the apocalyptic expectation, whether immediate or set in the future, gave converts a sense of mission and purpose, which no doubt added to the attractiveness.[41]

It can also be argued that the fall of Rome was indirectly a result of Christianity. Firstly, Paganism was banned in 394, which ended the worship of the traditional Roman pantheon.[42] Under this ban Augustus' Altar of Victory was removed from the Roman Senate House which many thought as a omen of the end.[43] One important key to start with is that of Christian faith. Christian faith encouraged worship and altruism and not pagan sacrifice. In addition, public and private wealth was spent for charity.[44] If Christianity pervaded the Roman culture then surely Christian ideals of modesty overcame the traditional Roman megalomania that aided in its survival.

Since the Roman Empire ruled over all the territory along the Mediterranean many cultures blended together and didn't produce favorable patriotism toward the pagan ideals of yesteryear. When turmoil over the various faiths mixed with the infamy of the Roman hierarchy wars broke out. To matters worse, Christian Rome started using public money for churches instead of expansion projects.[45]

My point here amongst all these historical references and cultural connections is that creativity, cultural transmission, and the need to control the masses has fabricated a monster out the human need to find ourselves in the universe. Religion is big business yet its just that, a business. Religious institutions adhere to Social Darwinism just as much as any other venture. History has revealed just how far, specifically Christianity, will go to gain a monopoly over human thought. Even political systems take example from religious plunders and usurp the masses. Its all an interesting study of how ideas mix together over time and are taken to an extreme by the reverent.

At this point in my discussion it seems appropriate to explore the diverse religions of the world in order to show the magnitude of human creativity. Keep in mind that originally religion is about answering metaphysical questions. Due to cultural and intellectual transformations the religious realm consists of more than just traditional sacred thought. There are many sects of

major religions and many parody religions
and yet still there are belief structures
that have survived from ancient times. I
will be brief and only impart the basics.

First off, the Vedas are among the oldest sacred texts generally thought to have
been composed between 1750 BCE and 600 BCE
and emerged in Indo-Europe.[46] The word Veda
is Sanskrit for "knowledge".[47] One main
aspect of Vedic followers before Hinduism
was ritual sacrifice.[48]

Hinduism is greatly influenced by the
Vedas and is considered by some to be the
oldest religion.[49] It is a polytheistic
faith but many believe that these gods are
just manifestations of a supreme power.[50]

Other religions loosely based on the
Vedas are Buddhism and Jainism. These two
religions were an answer to a religious
awakening in the 6th century BCE.[51] These
two supplied people with more personal mod-
els for life rather than sacrifices for the
priestly class(the Brahmins) that limited
freedom of thought.[52]

Buddhism's religious classification can
be called to question due the absence of the
idea of a creator God but nonetheless it is
a life philosophy oriented around the teachings of the Buddha. The Buddha lived and
taught in the northern India some time
between the 6th and 5th centuries BCE.[53]

As transmissions of thought and culture continued through time, Buddhism moved out of India into China and eventually into Japan merging with Taoism and Confucianism along the way to create what is called Zen Buddhism.[54] Taoism and Confucianism were especially popular and an integral part of Chinese culture when Buddhism arrived. Some have gone so far as to say that Buddhism became so popular in China due to Taoist connections to the other-worldly rather than the humanism of Confucianism.[55]

Overall, these Eastern religions have many sects and interpretations of orthodoxy too lengthy for my discussion.

Moving on, Western religions arose out of Zoroastrianism as I mentioned in "The Tempest Sea of Culture". Zoroaster did, how-ever, live and think in the Eastern world but it was his influence on the Hebrews that initiated the Abrahamic religions. According to Jewish tradition the Torah was revealed to Moses at Mount Sinai.[56] Jews ultimately view the five books of the Torah (the Old Testament Pentateuch) as having authoritative status because it expresses the covenant between God and the people of Israel.[57]

Outside of its central significance in Judaism, the Torah is accepted by Christianity as part of the Bible, compris-

ing the first five books of the Old
Testament. Moreover, Christianity alone has
countless denominations due to the shift in
social and political events over it's incep-
tion some mere 2000 years ago. The three
primary divisions of Christianity are Roman
Catholicism, Eastern Orthodoxy, and
Protestantism.[58] Protestantism is actually
an umbrella term for many non-Roman Western
Christians.[59] To put simply, Protestantism
is categorized into four confessional fami-
lies-Luthern, Anglican, Reformed, and Free
Church.[60] Interestingly enough, Haitian
Vodou is based upon a merging of the beliefs
and practices from such African countries as
the Kongo, Yoruba, and Fon with Roman
Catholicism that carried over from French
colonization.[61]

The Rastafari movement is a new religious movement loosely connected to
Christianity. Adherents believe that Haile
Selassie I, former Emperor of Ethiopia, as a
divine being and the champion of the black
race.[62] According to Rastafarians, blacks are
the Israelites reincarnated as punishment,
yet they will eventually be redeemed and
sent back to Africa where white people will
serve them.[63]

The third religion of the Abrahamic
religions is Islam. Muslims believe that
Islam is the complete and universal version

of a primordial faith that was revealed at
many times and places before, including
through Abraham and Jesus, whom they consider prophets.[64] Muslims maintain that previous messages and revelations have been par-
tially changed or corrupted over time, but
consider the Qur'an (meaning "recitation or
reading") to be both the unaltered and the
final revelation of God.[65] Muhammad is
regarded as the "Seal of Prophets", meaning
that he is considered to be the last prophet
of God.[66] Muhammad was born approximately in
the year 570 in Mecca.[67]

Lest I not forget to mention the many
pagan and new age religious movements. Of
the pagan religions still practiced there is
the matriarchal-based Wiccans[68] and the
patriarchal-based Satanism[69]. Both are
witchcraft related and use ideas spanning
centuries yet it hasn't been until recent
decades that they formed structured religions. Both are Earth-bound belief systems
yet Satanism is geared more toward being a
sophisticated animal through casting
spells[70] whereas Wiccans cast spells to har-
ness the secrets of nature[71].

The most famous of new age religions is
Scientology. Scientology is a body of
beliefs and related practices created by
speculative fiction author L. Ron Hubbard,
starting in 1952, as a successor to his ear-

lier self-help system, Dianetics.[72]
Scientology teaches that people are immortal
beings who have forgotten their true
nature.[73] Its method of spiritual rehabili-
tation is a type of counselling known as
auditing, in which practitioners aim to con-
sciously re-experience painful or traumatic
events in their past in order to free themselves of their limiting effects.[74]
Followers are known for opposing psychiatry,
and members are encouraged to cut off all
contact with material items in order to free
their souls of delusion.[75] By the way,
Scientologists believe that their
souls("thetans") reincarnate and have lived
on other planets before living on Earth.[76]

If all these religions weren't enough
to make your head spin read about these two
parody religions.

First there is the The Flying Spaghetti
Monster (FSM) which is the deity of what
started as the parody religion of the Church
of the Flying Spaghetti Monster or
Pastafarianism. The "Flying Spaghetti
Monster" first appeared in a satirical open
letter written by Bobby Henderson in 2005,
protesting the decision by the Kansas State
Board of Education to permit the teaching of
intelligent design as an alternative to evolution in public school science classes.[77]

In the letter, Henderson parodied the concept of intelligent design by professing belief in a supernatural creator that closely resembles spaghetti and meatballs.[78] Henderson further called for Flying Spaghetti Monsterism to be allotted equal time in science classrooms alongside intelligent design and evolution.[79] One of the many highlights of The Church of the Flying Spaghetti Monster is that Heaven features a Stripper Factory and a giant Beer Volcano.[80]

In addition to the FSM, there is The Invisible Pink Unicorn (IPU) which is the goddess of a parody religion used to satirize theistic beliefs. The IPU exists almost entirely on the internet.[81] On message boards some community members proscribe following all references to the IPU with BHHH, short for "bless her holy hooves," a play on the routinization of honorifics associated with religion and social elites.[82] The IPU takes the form of a unicorn that is paradoxically both invisible and pink. She is a rhetorical illustration used by religious skeptics as a contemporary version Carl Sagan's Invisible Dragon or Russell's teapot.[83] The Invisible Pink Unicorn is also sometimes mentioned in connection with The Flying Spaghetti Monster. The IPU is used to argue that supernatural beliefs are arbitrary by, for example, replacing the word

God in any theistic statement with Invisible
Pink Unicorn.[84] The mutually exclusive
attributes of pinkness and invisibility,
coupled with the inability to disprove the
IPU's existence, satirize properties that
some theists attribute to a theistic
deity.[85] Russell's teapot, by the way, is
an argument put forth by Bertrand Russell
that theories that cannot be proven false
must proven true by those who propose them
or be rejected.[86]

From the recesses of our philosophical
and creative archives comes many arguments
for and against an existence of a creator
and their supposed powers. Some argue on
the basis of ontology(which says that human
minds can't think of anything greater than
God) and some use the cosmological argu-
ment(there has to be a first cause for the
universe).[87] Freudians(who don't advocate
theist ideas) argue that God is like a much
needed father figure.[88] There is also agnos-
ticism, which states that there is no way to
really know whether God exists.[89]

In ethics there is the Divine Command
Theory which states that morality is based
on God's edict.[90] If God(namely the
Abrahamic God) has ultimate power overall
then killing innocent people is just because
He said so. This leads to the question of
whether might makes right.[91] Inquisitively,

if God is all powerful can he revamp his own proclamations? Can he change his mind and reorder the universe at whim? If so how can one take His orders as moral if it is hard to say what He really wants? And is it ultimately just to follow divine mandate out of fear?

Bare in mind that I didn't delve into the heated arguments of intelligent design versus evolution in this section. This topic is far too complicated to due to its politics to use in this book. However, in general, the redundant nature of the argumentative dialogue and the creativity of these theories does fit my notion of how humans endlessly search to answer metaphysical questions to sooth our mental stimulation, and due to the aforementioned underlining creativity and redundancy, humans need to sideline their dissent and compromise.

Through all these religious investigations I've realized that we have basically invented gods to sooth our human minds that are stressed and confused from interacting in society. We didn't know the answer so we invented one because our highly imaginative brains couldn't bare being without answers. Humans need hope mechanisms, theological existence, and metaphysical inquiry for solace and fulfillment. If not for the stresses of living as a human with other humans we wouldn't need the controlling effects of religion nor the mind quieting solutions easily put forth by our professed doctrines.

In addition, I think the monotheistic "God" is a symbol, not an objective thing in the cosmos, for how humans should act. We created this "God" out of the fantasy to be better than we are. It was the advent of the Judeo-Christian god that focused more on self transformation (spirituality) to sublimate animal urges in favor of altruism. This altruism was geared toward achieving the "Kingdom of Heaven" on Earth. Altering views argue about exactitude but basically Christianity aims for goodwill toward others and togetherness both of which don't exist in the animal kingdom. However, it was the hierarchy and power of religion that corrupted this dream into a lucrative, bloodthirsty business. Basically Christianity went from shunning animal urges to something greater then full circle back to acting like animals by which they compete with other religions and fight amongst themselves over the literal meaning of the bible.

It is the very corruptness and violent, hypocritical history that fills me with disdain for Christianity. On the other hand, the basis of the religion fits with my the-

sis-be compassionate to others and sublimate
animalistic behavior. Christian morals
should and can exist separate from the religion. The fact of the matter is that it
doesn't matter what Jesus said or what the
bible says or what some prophet says because
unity and care for others won't happen if
everyone is a religious fanatic. Fanaticism
leads to intolerance. Christian morality is
about the community and family, so keep
those values but loose the fundamentalism
that corrupts such ideals. To reiterate my
overall point in this paper-we are cognitive
beings and we have the power to over come
our animal instincts for the greater good of
humans and the legacy thereof.

    Fanaticism in general, but the "Kingdom
of Heaven" to be precise, reminds me of
Plato's allegory of the cave. It could be
said that this "kingdom" is just a vain
prison for oneself quarantined from the
intellect. Followers become indoctrinated
to such a degree that they will do anything
the bible says. Killing native peoples,
subduing women, enslaving people of different skin colors, refusing to allow medical
advances that may save lives but seem
immoral, and being adamant about the 10 com-
mandments that it infringes the separation
of church and state. The pious would rather
hide behind their literalism than actually

act kind to others and support a better
future world.

Friedrich Nietzsche said that,
"[Christianity is] the one immortal blemish
of mankind"[92], and I agree; however, I differ with Nietzsche on his promotion of the
"will to power". I in turn reverse everything in favor of the intellect. We are a
cognitive species. We shouldn't act barbaric. We should use our consciousness to make
the world better for everyone not just ourselves or our prized religion.

It seems to be habitual that people use
religion to control kids because religion is
an easy source to utilize. However, on the
one hand can kids really grasp the concept
of "God" as adults do? And is religion just
to scare kids with damnation? I've found
that most people who go through childhood in
a religious family grow up not questioning
their faith and just take it for fact. That
would be okay if the world became a more
peaceful place after all these generations
passing along religious virtue but where's
the peace? Somewhere in the process the
teaching and controlling of people through a
religious mindset has bequeathed an insur-
gence of turmoil. We humans get into our
minds some idea worth fighting for and eons
later forget why we started fighting but
continue to fight because we can't stop.

I've been asked whether I've read the bible. I haven't but that isn't the point. I know that those that ask that question of me are really wanting to know if I adhere to Christian morality. At which point I say that just through living and interacting one can learn not to steal, kill, cheat, or be vengeful so it defeats the purpose of holding the teachings of the bible on a pedestal. Through government laws one will get into major trouble financially if found guilty for a crime. Plus, reputations are destroyed, life's are ruined, and jobs are limited if one has a criminal record, so who needs religious doctrine when society itself will reciprocate with destructive power if control is lost. Therefore, "God" could also be a symbol for society. Society is in everything and everywhere and everything makes up society so do on to others as to avoid society's crippling affects.

Aren't all religions just an attempt at answering metaphysical questions? Why do religious wars exist if we can sift through history and find that religiosity is universal in beings who have cognizance of themselves and their surroundings? The major religions have immense power at their cores to coerce and usurp free thought so it's no wonder there exists such an uproar over

religious compromise. If such tumult pre-
sides with religion then isn't our desire
for world peace thwarted? If individual
sects of humans continue to hold different
truths for truth in opposition to other
individual belief systems then how can there
ever be compromise? All things considered,
religion has survived purely through random
cultural fusion, transmission of human creativity, and the animal urge to be in control and have power. Are we so confused by
our brains' mental activity that it makes us
so lonely and desperate that we construct a
unfathomable perfect being to comfort us
that we inevitably fight over its definition? Are we so enthralled existentially
that we resist nothing to find ultimate
truth about existence? Why can't we just be
and live in a world John Lennon imagined?

---The Evolved Predator Mechanisms that Usurp--

Human ruthlessness to others is no different than other animals on the personal track to survival, however humans use their enlarged frontal lobes and eclectic imagination to adapt to their (social) environments by creating more advanced and elusive tools for survival. Namely, we humans use research and technology to usurp others. It seems apparent to me that survival of the fittest doesn't apply to humans anymore but rather humans are in a tangle for the survival of the most powerful. Humans don't follow natural courses of evolution for adaptation they create their own rules of survival through manipulation and force. It is our complex existence in our cultural matrix that has lead to a definition of human that is beyond biology.

We have broken the chains of ecological classification. We are in a class of our own. Without our technology we would maintain our mammialian omnivorous environmental prison having to compete with other animals in a predator-prey system. Ironically, killing one another even after thousands of years of social development still perpetuates for the same time proven reasons. All our human made "weapons" are the very anti-utopian devices that are thwarting peace on this planet.

Weaponry, in its basic sense, has long since been a means at securing possessions and territory since ancient times. In this post industrial information age however with populations booming, the art of survival relys on technology and research to coerce others out of money and to secure lives with gadgets that aim at efficiently killing people and gaining power.

Our specialized division of labor sits at the center of this exploitative maelstrom. Knowledge is power, and those that have more experience and mastery in a field may not share their information in the hopes of vanity. Experienced entrepreneurs will hoard their secrets for self gain; mechanics know best how to extend a cars life; law makers, lawyers, and the police know the law better than anyone so they can exert power; computer techs know how and what gadgets are better; doctors know health related information; and it's the smart shopper who knows that money shouldn't be spent frivolously. Ultimately, it's every informed person with specialized knowledge that uses their wisdom as power over someone else to stay ahead.

What's more, with society becoming

bloated with people new marketing techniques
have had to be discovered in order to perpetuate the economy. Humans have found ways
to prey on others using psychological/mar-
keting research which makes us consume products we don't necessarily need so we become
unhealthy, confused, and acquire massive
amounts of stuff which we in turn then consume to remedy our problems. This creates
an emotional cycle of consuming or rather a
cycle of endless, multi-faceted stimulation.
Tapping human emotion is a lucrative business and is an evolved predator mechanism.
None of us are safe as long as we desire
things. If one is lost in a fog of bewilder-
ing neural activity chances are there is a
human made drug or procedure or peer group
outlet to subdue our problem back to normal-
cy. I say society experiments on our psyches to perpetuate society and no psychological avenue is off limits.

To start, it is marketing that generally finds ways to reach a target demographic
in order to advance commerce, and, interestingly enough, marketing is a science because
it involves the use of psychological, biological, and social discoveries to formulate
new paths of inquiry that aim to better
human lives. Unfortunately, marketers tend
to target two main psychological concepts

and exploit them. Satisfying customer needs
tends to besmirch cognizance by trickery.The
first is operant conditioning and the second
is the drive-reduction theory.

Operant conditioning is a type of
learning in which behavior is strengthened
if followed by reinforcement or diminished
if followed by punishment.[1] As consumers,
if a product is bought and is followed with
a pleasurable outcome then more than likely
the product with be bought again. In other
words, this initial process has had a positive reinforcement, and the consumer has
become "conditioned" to buy the product next
time. The fact of the matter is, the
greater the positive reinforcement, the
greater the likelihood of repeat purchase.

The drive-reduction theory, on the
other hand, states that a physiological need
creates an aroused state that drives the
organism to reduce that need.[2] In order to
beget drives is to encourage a revision of
the desired state: that is, getting the person to feel dissatisfied with the actual
state. Marketers usually target shifts in
the desired state as a means to their end
so they tailor their products to fit the
wide array of drives that people exhibit to
satisfy needs. Often, marketers try to get
people to satisfy drives with products they

don't need. In a sense, marketers set the
stage for people to complicate their lives
with material items that aren't necessary
for survival.

Say your wandering, slightly aimlessly,
through the grocery store, all the while
being price conscious about products, and
you hear a song that brings back fond memories or you smell a smell that does the same
and you suddenly find yourself buying the
product that elicits those memories. This
mystery behavior is the product of another
psychological trick called "atmospherics."

Atmospherics is the term used to define
the integration of store architecture,
color, sound, smell, layout, etc., that
manipulates the customer and orients them to
act in certain ways.[3] The sense of smell and
sight actually influence more consumer
behavior than anything due to the unconscious. In fact, the average person can
discriminate 4,000 to 10,000 different odor
molecules.[4] This ability to distinguish
odors is a product of evolution whereby
humans used smell to determine spoilage and
danger.[5] Moreover, smell became linked to
emotion and memory, so when an odor is present it may invoke pleasure, pain, or anger.[6]
Due to the overwhelming uncontrollibility of
consumer reactions to smell, marketers have

to mitigate their use of this tactic. Ultimately, the human sense of smell is about 10,000 times more sensitive than the human sense of taste.[7]

It is also said that the average product only gets one twenty-sixth of a second to attract our attention; therefore, making a product visually appealing is an huge obstacle for marketers to overcome in order to get there products seen.[8] In addition, reports inform that the warm colors (red, orange, and yellow) elicit the most stimulation on consumer behavior.[9]

If you thought having your emotions exploited and coerced into purchasing a product was bad check out my next example- "brand loyalty". Brand loyalty is when customers basically become attached to a certain brand and will most likely continue to purchase that brand.[10] Building brand equity is key to marketers who search for their niche and their identity. It has been noted that companies now plan "cradle-to-grave" advertising strategies hoping that nostalgic childhood memories of a brand will lead to a lifetime of purchases.[11] Some experienced business people believe that a person's brand loyalty may begin as early as the age of two.[12] Consequently, marketers have realized that loyal customers will spend more and that will, in turn, decrease marketing expenses. Business people of all kinds understand that it takes more to service and retain new customers than older ones. In fact, it costs at least five times as much to serve a new customer as an existing one.[13] Brand loyalty is, of course, conducive to exploitative behavior because marketers who have established loyal customers may tend to take advantage of them.

In essence, I think the individualist paradigm has gone too far with encouraging independence because people use up resources, get lazy, and eat food to fit their fast paced world which in turn isn't healthy. Food isn't food anymore, obesity is pervasive, and resources are dwindling, are these behaviors intelligent? We engage in behaviors because they make us feel good yet after extensive conditioning we cant break our bad habits. We find pleasure in the release of hormones and neurotransmitters so we get into the habit of consuming items that may be bad for us so long as we feel good.

If it weren't for hedonism we wouldn't have a economy responsible for spawning civilization. If you think about it, the Christmas season, fancy five-star restaurants, huge department stores and malls, and high-tech gadgets are all paragons of our opulent Western culture. Is it worth perpetuating society by creating an economy based on numerous capitalistic ventures that make people unhealthy and/or materialistic to the point that people become desolate and the world is polluted? All I'm saying is that people are molded to be consumers which leads those people to become gluttonous.

Moreover, it is the tyranny of individualism in our culture that incidentally becomes the despot by which everyone is ruled by. Tricking people to buy goods leads to employment which cycles back to support commerce, yet, take into account what the stresses of this despotic emotionally driven corrupting cycle do to people.

Smoking, as studies have found, will take 12 minutes or 4 hours off your life for every pack.[14] What's more, tobacco is the single greatest cause of preventable death globally.[15] Smoking tobacco leads most commonly to: lung cancer, heart disease, bronchitis, emphysema, cataracts, mouth cancer, pancreatic cancer, bone density loss, abdominal aortic aneurysm, brain aneurysm, and gastroesophageal reflux.[16] The effects depend on the number of years that a person smokes and on how much the person smokes. When tobacco is smoked, nicotine causes physical and psychological dependency. Nicotine triggers the release of the hormones epiphrine and norepinephrine, which in turn diminish appetite and boost alertness and mental efficiency.[17] Nicotine also stimulates the central nervous system to release neurotransmitters that calm anxiety and reduce sensitivity to pain.[18] Cigarette use by pregnant women has also been shown to cause birth defects, including mental and physical disabilities.[19]

Another aspect of stress involves disruptions in sleep. In humans, sleep deprivation suppresses immune cells that fight off viral infections and cancer, which helps explain why people who sleep 8 hours a night tend to outlive those chronically sleep deprived.[20] Chronic sleep debts also alter metabolic and hormonal functioning in ways that mimic aging and are conducive to obesity, hypertension, and memory impairment.[21]

With the tendency for McDonaldization people move without haste and accelerate their lives to such a degree that laudable food choices are side-lined. About 90% of the money that Americans spend on food is used to buy processed food.[22] In addition, Americans drink soda at an annual rate of about 56 gallons per person-that's nearly 600 12-oz cans of soda per person.[23]

Compared with their counterparts in the early 1900s, people are eating a higher fat, higher sugar diet, expending fewer calories, and suffering more diabetes at younger ages.[24] The sickness of today's eating disorders lies not just within the victims but also within or weight obsessed culture that says "Fat is bad", which motivates millions of women to be dieting and that encourages eating binges by pressuring women to live in a constant state of semistarvation.[25] Obesity is 6 times more common among lower class than upper class women, more common among Americans than Europeans, and more common among Americans today than in 1900.[26] When Eric Schlosser wrote <u>Fast Food Nation</u> in 2002 it was noted that more than half of all American adults and about one-quarter of all American children were obese or overweight.[27]

Are we to let society stress us out so that we kill ourselves through self destructive behavior while in the meantime creating jobs and transferring money that perpetuates the economy? It's as if the means(being emotionally manipulated) justified the end(prolonging society).

Aside from the vicious psychological marketing tactics that yield death and decay, we humans exercise our technology to survive beyond any genetic predispositions through another evolved predator mechanism-basic weapons. As previously stated, humans don't follow natural courses of evolution for adaptation they create their own rules of survival through force. At a glance, the most genetically ill-equipped person can out live a genetical healthy and strong individual as easy as a pull of a trigger.

The arsenal of weapons humans have invented just in the past 100 years ranges from mechanized warfare to nuclear.[28] Poison gas was first used in 1915 and tanks first appeared in 1916.[29] In addition, submarines were first used by the Germans during WW1.[30] Stealth is a new technology that tries to reduce radar signatures.[31] It wasn't until the 1960s and 1970s that carbon-fibre composites and high-strength plastics made it possible to make aircraft either complexly curved or flat.[32] A nuclear weapon is an explosive device that derives its destructive force from nuclear reactions, either fission or a combination of fission and fusion.[33] These devices can yield a destructive force well into the megatons of TNT.[34]

How is it that so many religions preach pacifism and so many people desire peace on

Earth yet governments across the globe endlessly engage in war? In fact, it is estimated that anywhere from 150 million to 1
billion people have been killed in wars
throughout history.[35] Interestingly, wars
reduce birthrate by sending men to battle.
It is estimated that WW11 caused a population deficit of at least 20 million.[36]

War is also expensive. From 1940 to
1996, America spent $16.23 trillion on the
military.[37] In addition, U.S. arms manufac-
turers, in 2001, exported $9.7 billion in
weapons worldwide.[38]

Despite opinions about the usefulness
of war, pragmatic pacifism holds that the
costs of war and inter-personal violence are
so substantial that better ways of resolving
disputes must be found. It seems such a
waste to pile up the dead and spend a gar-
gantuan amount of money on territorial and
economic vanity instead of on healthcare and
education.

In the states there is in fact a growing amount of legislation concerning guns
and violence. Some laws protect and some
restrict but all in all it is the laws that
restrict that anger the people the most.
Why? The answer is simple: people don't want
to evolve past their innate survival tactics. People would rather simply kill some-

one than work out an issue or compromise. Before we can evolve past ego protection we need to focus on the many reasons that encourage individuals to commit crimes. Again, people are afraid of everything and having weapons eases that tension. Not to mention the fact that as the economy suffers peoples' finances suffer resulting in drastic measures of survival.

One scary piece of legislation that stems from current panophobic tendencies is the "Make my Day" law. It states that, "any occupant of a dwelling is justified in using any degree of physical force, including deadly physical force, against another person when that other person has made an unlawful entry into a dwelling, and when the occupant has reasonable belief that such other person has committed a crime in the dwelling in addition to uninvited entry, or is committing or intends to commit a crime against a person or property in addition to the univited entry, and when the occupant reasonably believes that such other person might use any physical force, no matter how slight, against any occupant."[39] This law continues by stating, "any occupant of a dwelling using physical force, including deadly physical force, in accordance with the provisions of subsection (2)of this section [the aforementioned section] shall be immune from any civil liability for injuries or death resulting from the use of such force."[40]

It is this savage quest to carve oneself a niche in the world that leads to all the rancor and malevolence in the world. The "Make my Day" law just goes to show how far people will go in desperate measures to keep themselves secure, and how society is so willing to adopt such legislation out of fear.

You may be thinking to yourself that I'm forgetting about all the medical advances and economic recoveries that have resulted from war not to mention the foundations of many nations including our own. No, I haven't disregarded those elements. I left that history lesson out because my point is that the world is at a crux where everything that humans stand for can be destroyed in a matter of seconds. Furthermore, there are enough separate science sectors in the world that war isn't necessary for advances. In addition, our leading research labs aren't under a religious iron grip like centuries ago so scientists can continue their studies without fear of excommunication.

Ok so now you're probably wondering about the problem of deterring and detaining

people in an utopia. Capital punishment has
existed in many forms since the dawn of civilization. Everything from cutting fingers
and limbs off to being drawn and quartered
to being burned alive to electrocution.
Ultimately, it has been human error and
issues with social structure that have
resulted in most crime.

When some people have money and luxuries and others don't the disadvantaged tend
to take action. When the law protects the
people who have money and power the disadvantaged take law in their own hands. When
society makes everything cost money but hin-
ders employment then, again, the desolate
take matters into their own hands. How are
we to reform the world into equality without
the repetition of revolutions and political
corruption?

In a society of intelligence we could
weed out genetically crime-prone personali-
ties using eugenics and cellular coding.
That thought alone may induce so many ethical concerns that you would rather live in a
decaying world than play "God". These are my
most sci-fi, quixotic thoughts and remember
they're just thoughts. However, we as
humans uphold a definition of human that is
beyond biology, like I mentioned earlier in
this chapter, so anything that is beyond
mere nature is human and therefore up for

utility. In other words, we have the technology at hand, due to our un-naturalness as
advanced beings, so why not modify ourselves
by any means to make us better? Why not
use our scientific knowledge to mold us out
of nature's randomness to eliminate crime,
violence, war, and anything else. This goes
for the ethics of abortion(in terms of personhood I say personhood starts when a human
gets socialized to interact in the world.
I'm pro choice/pro child/anti-child if that
makes any sense. In other words, people have
the choice despite religious doctrine
because it is their bodies, once the decision has been made to keep a child a raise
them then responsibility should be given,
and we should try to limit population growth
to limit pollution and suffering) and
euthanasia as well. If people decide not to
have kids after pregnancy then it shouldn't
be demonized. And if people decide they
want to die then they should be granted that
choice. We humans act like no other species
which makes us superior, so if we can we
should, or if we choose our choice should be
honored.

We could also institute a means of giving every child an education, change cur-
riculums so all ages learn the same material, reduce outside distractions that yeild
drop outs. I propose more ponderables to

create an intelligent peaceful society in "Nascent Omniscience".

All in all, in times of past we have waged wars and committed violent acts to conquer territory under seemingly malicious and extrinsic means but now the world needs to mesh all cultures and equate prosperity and unlearn prejudice. Sure revolutions have been necessary in times of yore and unfortunately in times of present desolation, but isn't the human species beyond the need for war or economic despotism? What is done is done. We can't rewind time and prevent slavery, genocide, torture, segregation of skin color, and the mistreatment of native peoples by colonists and capitalists. We can entertain ourselves with counterfactuals until the cows come home but it won't change anything. What we got to think about is what future historiographers will think about us. There might not be any future historiographers if we blow ourselves up, but say we do prolong the human civilization what will the questions be like? Will the future ask why we didn't just stop fighting one day or will they ask what prevented us from noticing our self-destruction earlier in world history? Can't intellectual diplomacy be a panacea? Can't the pen be mightier than the sword?

Nascent Omniscience

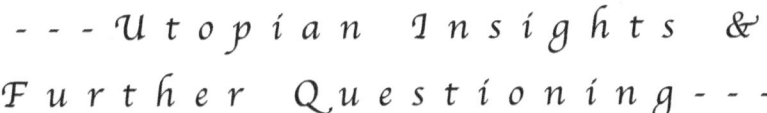

" Wisdom is a dreadful thing when it brings no profit to its possessor"-Sophocles(Oedipus Rex)

As another thought experiment look at the mountains and imagine what those gigantic piles of rocks would say if they could talk. Note that they have been around for millions of years, so if they could talk they could express their opinion of the changing landscape, of ecological evolution, of time itself, and of how humans constantly are ego-prone and stop at nothing to recreate and exploit the natural environment. They would have also experienced first hand the developments of white people oppressing natives, of diseases, of wars, and of changing cultural trends. I bet the mountains are laughing at us. They are the ultimate Zen masters who know the truth yet sit back and watch our human odysseys.

Also, less pessimistically, mountains release a timeless sensation that is almost mystifying. Mountains, and trees the like, exist carefree and serene and content to whatever nature throws at them, give it wind, cold, heat, or the destructive force of a species. One Taoist expression sums up this idea: "Whoever is stiff and inflexible is a disciple of death. Whoever is soft and yielding is a disciple of life."[1] In other words, one should aspire to be less lavish and less tense and more stoic and blithe. Throw out all cultural ties and the stressful rigor of daily self preservation and meditate on the eternal unknown of the cosmos.

My idea of nascent omniscience, in fact, fits loosely with the Zen Buddhist concept of prajna. Prajna being defined as a transcendental wisdom. In act this is an overcoming of ego with compassion for synergy with nature. It is both an act of intellectual will and of not thinking.[2]

There is, on the other hand, a trend to live as a hedonist which seems to be an extreme that isn't virtuous. Opponents such as Aristotle and Confucius called for a mean between excesses and deficits.[3] Simply put, this mean states that living modestly with

reason is more fulfilling and lasts longer
over time instead of seeking endless pleasure as a standard of life's purpose. In
addition, it's our character not our actions
that ultimately make lives better in social
arenas. To act with virtue toward one
another is reciprocal. I've always thought
that if one strived for a long life of
virtue then more wisdom would be acquired,
self-actualization would arise, moral turpi-
tude would decrease, and a greater apprecia-
tion of existence would out weigh frivolous
self-destructive pleasure seeking. These
"carpe-diem types"(as I refer to them) constantly claim that one can't take money and
wealth beyond the grave so we should live
for the day as if it's our last. However,
one must be aware that we can't take the
joys and experiences of life with us either.
     Ephemerality is pervasive as a human
and the pleasures at hand seem to good to
pass up, but shouldn't we as a species
strive for greater tomorrows by being virtuous today? We should have a collective con-
scientious toward our legacy by limiting our
excesses. Our god wars should end and come
together to unite for a common objective.
We don't need a metaphysical ideal but
rather a universal, down-to-earth concern
for humanity through modesty and restrictive
behavior. Maybe even our heart felt so-

called democracies will have to end and become more fascist in order to limit human error. Sure having inalienable rights sounds just but remember the Enlightenment occurred in a time before a billion people roamed the Earth and before the advent of the Industrial Revolution. In fact the world didn't reach a billion inhabitants until 1800 once medicical advances decreased mortality rates.[4] In the end, we are at a crossroads with global change to accomodate masses of people on one hand and dealing with traditional ego enhancements on the other.

Several elements to remedy our situation are on the drawing board for consideration, but one must also consider the past as evidence for possible outcomes that should be avoided. For instance, Jared Diamond and Joseph A. Tainter have both written about historical events in the past that have caused the collapse of civilization.[5] Basically both books boil down to a few simple elements. First, water is needed to survive. Water keeps our bodies hydrated and our food growing. At our current rate at the current time we might face a new water crisis given increasing amounts of population. It has been argued that previous civilizations have collapsed because of population growth that exceeds the capacity

of the environment and thus water became
short in supply. If populations increase
dramatically, like they have been, food will
be harder to grow because there will be less
land and there will be more overhead cost
for growing the food. Farmers, of today,
are already experiencing some tough decisions. Some in the desert regions of
California have had to ruin age old crops
because the cost too much to keep them due
rising water costs.

Secondly, we can't depend on the fuels
that we use, yet fossil fuels are most powerful. It has been noted by the ecological
footprint that the American lifestyle
requires as much as 9.5 hectares per person,
and if everyone on the planet lived like
Americans it would require 5 Earths.[6] Scary
thought when faced with the idea about making future generation greater than the previous. What's more, the total global demand
is 2.2 hectares whereas total global supply
is 1.8 hectares making demand exceed supply
by 20%.[7]

Third, we can't live raffishly with all
our excesses because pollution is changing
the atmosphere and causing(and might
increase to cause) water levels to increase
and flooding to happen.

And finally, we can't be so violent
toward one another. Albeit wars have creat-

ed a revampment of society in the past, the fact is that wars are expensive and just further disagreements. Both authors contend that humans need to learn from the past and focus on the now instead of engaging in ego-trips.

Our change will be a major social undertaking. We need to halt population growth, we need to moderate our excesses, and we need to halt religious dissent. Too much violence has been begotten by religious indifference, and because of population growth pollution is ruining our fabulous life-sustaining planet. If we continue on this path of natural destruction and war mongering, society will collapse and revert all back to nature. On the other hand, if humans instead resort to nuclear holocaust then the Earth will also be forever jaded. Either way people will have to rebuild civilization from scratch if we refuse to let go of our luxuries and ignorance toward population growth.

The proclivity toward Anthropocentrism only bolsters the fact that humans are a teleologically-absorbed, fiendishly sex oriented species that through eons of neural evolution have fabricated a highly imaginative matrix of solipsistic and dissentful pandemonium. We are at the pinnacle of humanity yet animal mannerisms are holding us back, i.e.: seven deadly sins. Why can't humanity breach this obstacle? What is the human race going to actually do with all our knowledge? Better yet why do we need billions of people on the planet if we can't sustain all that life. There isn't enough resources for everyone to live like an American. We need to make life pleasant for everyone and not have tycoons hoarding all the wealth.

I've always been fascinated with the wisdom of the elderly and research shows that one key to becoming a centenarian is to manage stress.[8] So in order to construct a utopian culture where ego is homogenized for utilitarian means we need to limit stress in all sectors of life (Refer to my discussion of stress and the "Individualist paradigm" in "Purpose Decay"). It just makes sense to make everyone healthier and live fulfilling lives.

Interestingly enough, Eastern sages and Yogis have a honed knowledge on the effects of breathing.[9] Some can slow their heart rate down to one beat per minute which allows them to feel no pain and meditate with tremendous intensity.[10] Moreover, it has been said that some practitioners can stop breathing altogether and can be buried alive.[11] Overall, it is thought by these

sages that people have a set number of
breathes given to us, so we shouldn't waste
breathes being anxious, angry, or overly
emotional.[12]

If we as a species dream of world peace
we need to resolve issues dealing with the
horrors of how millions of people starve in
third world countries, how tons of people
can't afford health care, and how a low per-
centage of people are rich beyond their
wildest imaginations but are so caught up in
their fantasies that they become apathetic
toward the rest of the world. The question
at hand is do we either decide to restrict
the population or do we find better ways to
accommodate everyone? I think one thing is
for certain everything will change whether
we like it or not. We can't continue at
our current propulsion. People can't get
competitive over possessions and traditions.
We need to find a way to compromise for the
greater good of humanity. Redundant arguments get no where when everyone thinks they
have the right answer.

Most importantly, and this is key in my
opinion, we know what stages a child's brain
goes through during development, so we
should utilize that plasticity and teach (or
not teach some things) that will result in a
society less full of bias. I've always
thought about expanding the slight progres-

sion of standardized critical thinking
classes that exist in primary school and
instead start teaching philosophy(including
sociology, anthropology, and psychology)
early on. Of course the material would have
to be suitable for young kids but exposing
children to a multitude of different views
would lessen prejudice of perspective.
Teaching our progeny early on that subjectivity and compassion for alternate views
will lead to a more humanitarian world is
good. In addition, those that choose to procreate need to be sure to establish an
enriching and worldly environment for the
newborn. People shouldn't mindlessly have
children unless absolutely certain that the
child will grow up with security and opportunity.

If humans are to progress to extra terrestrial habitats we need to actually share
resources and master our territory and we
should play god if we are to be and continue
to be an intelligent species capable of modifying our environment and lifespans.
Manipulating cells, experimenting with therapies, advancing medicines that aid in survival is very human. I think we have to
think about spreading our technology to the
underdeveloped countries and spread humanitarian ideals across the globe. What's more,
I think this "green" revolution will eventu-

ally upgrade our control of the Earth and move us toward a more harmonious existence with our fellow humans.

At this point I find it relevant to discuss the Anthropic Principle as a show-case of synergism. This priniciple presents evidences of homeostatic situations or Goldilocks zones.[13] Here are some examples contained in The Anthropic Principle:

- the Earth has liquid water whereas liquid water has yet to be found elsewhere in the universe

- the moon stabilizes our axis

- if nuclear fusion forces were weaker or stronger then protons and neutrons would run amuck and wouldn't have combined with others resulting in the formation of ele-ments and eventually matter

The full list is rather arcane and scholarly and ment only for the most pious of physicists, cosmologists, biologists, and researchers to ponder.

Interestingly enough, something as sim-ple and small as a honeybee disappearing can throw the world off economic balance. The documentary Vanishing of the Bees[14] explains how bees pollinate all types of plants which lend to the countless varities of fruits and vegetables, and if these bees vanish then our food stuffs will dissipate as well, not to mention the livlihoods of farmers. Come to find out, the chemicals that farmers put on their crops to thwart insect infestation also tampered with the bees' natural courses. What's more, genetically modifying crops and or having one crop on a field instead of several plants species also limited bee congregations.

Although these last few paragraphs contain an interesting array of data, my aim here was to reveal some facts about the delicate balance of nature and how humans should find a life philosophy similar to Taoism to cause a metamorphosis of the world's denizens in order to create a new world culture.

Despite altering views on the superfluous and metaphysical, once we die we never exist again as the current form and with the current capacities as we do now, so I suggest that our aim, or purpose rather, is just to affect the world for good. Since our dawn as a questioning species with time to focus on other activities besides just survival, humans have asked "why are we here?" I say we are what we are and we should just be beings that use our innate capacities for intelligence. We should live creatively and harmoniously. Enjoy the pleasure giving pleasure centers of the brain, but don't take for granted ephemerality or the future.

In addition to natural harmony, there's
a theoretical scale proposed by Nikolai
Kardashev, a Soviet Russian astronomer, that
measures the progression of civilization
that epitomizes my idea. The rightly named
"Kardashev Scale" puts energy consumption of
an entire civilization in a cosmic perspective and has three designated categories
called Type I, II, and III.[15] These are
based on the amount of usable energy a civilization has at its disposal, and the degree
of space colonization. In general terms, a
Type I civilization has achieved mastery of
the resources of its home planet, Type II
harnesses the energy output of a star, and
generates about 10 billion times the energy
output of a Type I civilization, and Type
III of its galaxy or about 10 billion time
the energy output of a Type II
civilization.[16] The current human civilization is a Type 0 civilization, which means
we use energy from dead plants (i.e. oil and
coal).[17] Some calculations suggest we may
attain Type I status in about 100-200 years,
Type II status in a few thousand years, and
Type III status in about 100,000 to a million years.[18]

If we are to attain such grandiose levels of civilization we need not stratify
people based on prejudice or restrict legis-
lature that could possibly open doors to a

better society. For example, if by incorpo-
rating socialist ideas we could share wealth
and make everyone's lives more enjoyable.
Albeit lavishness would be out of the question and we know how bad people love their
excesses. My stance here sounds very liberal
but conservativism is a problem. Retaining
traditional viewpoints leads to intolerance
of other views and one can't grow intellec-
tually in those situations. We need to teach
understanding. We need to teach what religion has tried but failed at and that's compassion. We need to teach that every human
is made of the same material and we all suffer in times of desolation. We need to teach
that human cognizance is a powerful thing
and we should use that power to achieve the
peace that everyone dreams of. Sure there
will be issues with an utopian society con-
sisting of equality and opportunity for all
but isn't that the goal that humans have
subconsciously aimed for since the dawn of
civilization?

Pacifism is another facet that may have
to be institutionalized. I realize that
pacifism is a dirty word to all the aggressive types in the world because one thinks
one needs to be aggressive to survive.
However, that notion alone is also an issue.
This idea leads to violence, i.e., revenge,
hostility, and mutiny. Humor me for one

moment and consider an attribute on anar-
chist thought. Anarchists routinely say
that it is the fact that we have possessions
that initiates the desire for others to use
force to attain those possessions, hence the
advent of self-protection and the police.
Take this a step higher and the military
enters the picture. Anyway, whereas
Anarchists use this idea to justify forceful
change I'm using it to reiterate how our
world got to where it is. Essentially its is
our delusions of grandeur that cause our own
destruction. Wars are waged in the name of
opposing religions, neighbors fight neighbors over land, people argue over the exactitude of laws(and usually exploit the law
for self-gain), and people ultimately fight
if they feel they've lost control. These are
all just ideas. It's these ideas that we are
really fighting to preserve. In turn, a
group's military is just organized crime to
protect the ideas of that group. I'm not
denouncing the military(especially the U.S.
military) because without it the world's
tyrants would run amuck. I'm just saying
that it's our need to protect ourselves from
others out of fear that has required the
militaries and law enforcement agencies of
the world to exist, and violence in general.
    If we continue on this path of natural
destruction and war mongering society will

collapse and revert all back to nature. If nuclear holocaust ever happens and humans somehow survive the Earth will exhibit different ecological behavior and people will have to rebuild civilization all over again. Do we want that to happen? Do we want history to repeat wherein bias and control conquers dissent by engaging in ethnocentric behavior and destruction? Are we going to continue to litter the history books with stories about religious fanaticism, culture wars and blight, gender bias, and all out rash anthropocentric decisions that justify manipulation and death. Ultimately, in this world of socio-political Hydras, the products of history and tradition have become the many heads that need to be decapitated in order to change the future, progress our civilization, and actualize the wet-dream of peace that is so ubiquitous in world religions and the human legacy.

Epilogue

---Redundant Manifestations---

There are several instances of redundancy in my writing. And actually redundancy by itself is an idea I repeat. In "The Tempest Sea of Culture" I talk about how dialogue and drama is a redundancy of the human condition. In "The Predator Mechanisms that Usurp" I mention how war and violence have occurred throughout history. In "Created Concepts" I always came back to creativity and imagination as the sources for our self-made world. In "The Feeble Safeguards of Longevity" I expressed the tireless, ill-fated attempts at controlling nature. A lot of sections discussed how we have cognizance but can't seem to control our err. In addition, I ultimately talked about how humans are beyond nature because we have made our own environment.

I remember when I first came across redundancies. It all goes back to when Manursive was a creative force. After we made <u>OmniNecroVore</u> the idea to get serious and get a fanbase was stirring. One member knew an up-and-coming band and he posited the notion that we should make music that was popular in the metal scene. After a few discussions we couldn't agree so out of creative differences the band broke up. This event inspired me to write a poem that expressed my disdain for the types of people who blindly go for fame. The poem is called "Your Fantasy" and I wrote it in 2003:

> To each his own,
> A look of comfort.
> Images framed by dreams.
> Visions to corrupt and rearrange.
> Heed any experience
> To mold life's many schemes.
>
> Epidemic testimony with concerns to rule the world
> Failure lies in the process.
> Snapshots like a seed.
> Things happen for a reason,
> United with turmoil in between,
> And your invited to live up to your fantasies
>
> Lewd behavior outbursts
> Due to the extent of your thirst.
> Virtuous blithe,
> Tediously aghast.
> Learn to sacrifice,
> Benign or benighted by vice.

Sacred thoughts remind you of your goal,
To pick and choose your efforts
Before you sell your soul.
Cry out for help
And shadows come to play.
Juvenile grace into psyche damage
Anxiously desired for the inspiration of majesty.
Upon the zenith your invited
To corrupt and rearrange your fantasy.

With no band to show my poems to I just started randomly writing poems with roughly this same style. I call my poetry Dada poetry because I don't really follow any meter and I just put words or fragmented thoughts as lines. I think my style invokes thought but even I don't know remember exactly what I was thinking after the fact.

I'll give another example of my verbose Dada poetry. This time the year was 2007 and I was working two jobs and was really stressed and full of questions. In it I reference chaos theory, dating, sociology, and I also use imagery of all sorts. What I do know is that I was thinking about about how humans constantly crave answers, which is redundant, and how we constantly add to things, which is also redundant. The poem is called "And":

Drones and throngs meander about in lunacy,

Expressing drivel and coveting "why".
Animated pendulums swing,
As genres of tragedy recur in abundance.
This metronome of plagiarized language
Escapes the vines of neural insight,
These of which are imprisioned by banks of tradition

In avante garde obscurity,
A matrix of sounds and pathways
Condition minds to norms of culture.

When butterflies are flapping their wings,
The Earth turns in complexity.
A science of new age discoveries,
Pulls the strings of silence
Unleashing discomfort and ego.

Groundhogs burrowing mirror our assumptions.
An avalanche of convictions don't move mountains,
But prey like vampires afraid of the sun-
Usurping innocent souls.

Dating game rituals and poetic stanzas
Happen out of an eternal nebula.
Codes and signs name the phenomena of morality.
Deterministic systems repeat,
A cyclical dream toward a knowledge of "and".

Sometimes I get really annoyed with
redundancy and want to engage in apan-
thropinization in order to quell my

thoughts. For instance, I regularly look at
the opposite sex with the knowledge that I'm
suppose to be attracted to them but, as I
talked about in "The Cauldron of Scientific
Entities", I'm socialized to be stimulated
by images that fit the standard of beauty.
Plus, anatomy has revealed that the human
body is not only complex but an amalgam of
blood and guts, so what am I suppose to be
attracted to? Sometimes due to these
thoughts I have asexual tendencies because
to me people are just animate piles of cells
that produce waste, contain bacteria, and
live in ignorance of a world that is human
made. It's like humans are walking petri
dishes with culture. I find that the paradox
of us humans being intelligent creatures and
yet exhibiting the very attributes of lower
animals is just mind boggling. It just
amazes me that humans have existed as long
as they have. Of course if everyone thought
the human body was disturbing then people
wouldn't procreate. To make matters worse,
I even get annoyed with having to dispose of
waste because I know I will eventually have
to eat again which repeats the cycle. I
guess I'm too misanthropic and nihilistic to
see the excitement of hollow adventures and
pleasures.

Drama and dialogue are also redundant
fixtures of the human condition. People talk

and then generations later people talk about
the same thing then generations after that
the same things are still being discussed.
Why must people always and eternally talk
about the sensations their bodies are going
through, what they think someone else's
opinion is, how to gain power, what the
meaning of life is, what cultural trends
should be followed, how works sucks, or how
pleasure is going to be had in some future
moment? People always act the same in certain situations as well. For example, when
people are stressed they respond to questions hastily and with attitude. Moreover,
people try to give advice based on their own
experiences yet those personal experiences
don't always fit with another's personal
situation. In this case people jump to conclusions without considering the whole
story. The context of each perspective needs
to be evaluated before opinions and action
can be executed. And ultimately, people
don't like being wrong. Humans generally
tend to take offense when their egos are
questioned.

Philosophy itself is a redundancy in my
mind. Since the institution of agriculture
humans have had free time to ponder existence, so everyone from Socrates to Sartre
have engaged in an act that stems from the
boredom of free time as a product of agri-

culture. It's all just human creativity and imagination. It's this creativity that makes people prone to get in trouble. In other words, when given enough free time people routinely break rules and challenge the system. Religion is also a consequence of philosophical musings. Spirituality has found its niche in humans who continuously seek answers and desire hope. The neural pathways of human cognizance are astounding yet when combined with populations and time such powers become haphazard, contextless, and ill-fated.

This odyssey through the archives of humanity has been insightful to say the least. I have covered just about everything from atoms to war. As I read over this work I find that topics overlap and I end up cross referencing myself. This actually makes sense because when dealing with complexities of humanity one topic is bound to overlap another. I did try to section ideas off as best as possible, however to clarify a few points I've made I'm writing this epilogue.

My overall aim in this book was to write the philosophy book I've always wanted to read. Moreover, I've read books with a lot of fluff in them in order to fill pages and I set out not to do that. Unfortunately, this book is really small. Mind you, I could've made this book huge but it would've taken a tremendous amount of time to discuss every aspect of humanity that involves intelligence, human error, ego, exploitation, manipulation, and the zillion theories out there.

If every word in every sentence in this manifesto is a product of my mind's adaption to my personal experiences throughout my life then can it be said that I'm a solipsist. I mean, if these are my words expressed my way and no other person came to these conclusions, then am I a lone observer peering through lenses of my self made self? Sure one would think there is an outside world external to the mind but is there? Everything the world supposedly does to our neural pathways is only comprehended by our brains, so our brain is the creator of what we think we experience. My brain has created a sense of "me". If you exist then your brain created "you" and I am just a figment in your intricate dimension. If these musings hold, is this writing a work about humans being a complicated creature of epic stature or is this writing a reflection of me as a creature?...

- Credits -

Preface-
    1 The Matrix. Directed by Andy and Larry
Wachowski. Featuring Keanu Reeves and Laurence
Fishburne. Warner Bros, 1999.
    2 Official Website of the Ossuary In Kutna Hora -
Sedlec. http://www.kostnice.cz/

The Synthesis of the Archives-
    Created Concepts:
    1 "Biological Sciences: Taxonomy". The New
Encyclopaedia Britannica. 15th ed. vol 14. 2002.
    2 "Geologic Time". The New Encyclopaedia
Britannica. 15th ed. vol 5. 2002.
    3 Kelly, Eugene. The Basics of Western Philosophy.
Greenwood Press, 2004. page 50.
    4 Ibid. page 189-198.
    5 Diamond, Jared. Guns, Germs, and Steel: The
Fates of Human Societies. New York: Norton, 1999.
    6 Myers, David G. Exploring Psychology Fifth Edition
in Modules. New York: Worth Publishers, 2003.
    7 Ibid.
    8 Velasquez, Manuel. Philosophy: A Text with
Readings. Wadsworth Group, 2002. page 278.

    The Tempest Sea of Culture:
    1 Johnson, Allan G. The Blackwell Dictionary of
Sociology: A User's Guide to Sociological Language.
Blackwell Publishers Ltd, 1995.
    2 Breidenbach, Joana and Pal Nyiri. Seeing Culture
Everywhere: from Genocide to Consumer Habits. University

of Washington Press, 2009. pages 21-22.

3 Fiero, Gloria K. <u>The Humanistic Tradition:</u>
<u>Prehistory to the Early Modern World.</u> 4th Ed. New York:
McGraw Hill. 2002. page 4.

4 Ibid.

5 Ibid. page 10.

6 Ibid.

7 Ibid. page 37.

8 Ibid. page 36.

9 Ibid.

10 Dawkins, Richard. <u>The God Delusion</u>.New York:
First Mariner Books, 2006. page 51.

11 Fiero, Gloria K. <u>The Humanistic Tradition:</u>
<u>Prehistory to the Early Modern World.</u> 4th Ed. New York:
McGraw Hill. 2002. page 46.

12 Ibid. page 56.

13 Ibid.

14 Ibid. page 30.

15 Wolf, Naomi. <u>The Beauty Myth: How Images of</u>
<u>Beauty Are Used Against Women</u>. Harper Perennial, 2002.

16 Ibid.

17 Ibid.

18 Gilmore, David D.. <u>Misogyny: the Male Malady</u>.
Philadelphia: University of Pennsylvania Press, 2001.

19 Ibid.

20 Ibid.

21 Ibid.

22 Ibid.

23 Ibid.

24 Ibid.

25 Marsa, Linda. "She Thinks, He Thinks". <u>Discover:</u>
<u>The Brain</u>. Spring 2007.

26 Ibid.

27 Ibid.

28 Page, Jake. <u>Dogs: A Natural History</u>. New York: HarperCollins Publishers Inc., 2007.

29 Ibid.

30 Ibid.

31 Ibid.

Of Masks & Masochism:

1 Frankl, Viktor E.. <u>Man's Search for Meaning</u>. Beacon Press, 1959. page 125.

2 <u>Modify</u>. Dir Jason Gary. Committed Films, LLC. 2005.

The Feeble safeguards of Longevity:

1 Blue Oyster Cult. "Godzilla". <u>Spectres</u>. Columbia Records, 1977.

2 "Seven Wonders of the World". <u>The New Encyclopaedia Britannica</u>. 15th ed. vol 10. 2002.

3 "Zeus, Statue of". <u>The New Encyclopaedia Britannica</u>. 15th ed vol 12. 2002.

4 Flexner, Stuart and Doris Flexner. <u>The Pessimist's Guide to History</u>. Quill, 2000. page 8.

5 "Halicarnassus, Mausoleum of". <u>The New Encyclopaedia Britannica</u>. 15th ed vol 5. 2002.

6 "Rhodes, Colossus of". <u>The New Encyclopaedia Britannica</u>. 15th ed vol 10. 2002.

7 Romer, John and Elizabeth Romer. <u>The Seven Wonders of the World: A History of the Modern Imagination</u>. New York: Henry Holt and Company, Inc., 1995. page 55.

8 "Artemis, Temple of". <u>The New Encyclopaedia Britannica</u>. 15th ed vol 1. 2002.

9 "Giza, Pyramids of". <u>The New Encyclopaedia</u>

<u>Britannica</u>. 15th ed vol 5. 2002.

10 "Grand Canyon". The World Book Encyclopedia. World Book, Inc., 2000.

11 <u>Life After People: The Series</u>. Produced by Flight 33 Productions, LLC for History. A&E Television Networks, 2009-2010.

The Cauldron of Scientific Entities:

1 Angelo, Joseph A, Jr. <u>Encyclopedia of Space and Astronomy</u>. New York: Facts on File, Inc., 2006.

2 Clark, Stuart. <u>Stars and Atoms: From the Big Bang to the Solar System</u>. New York: Oxford University Press, 2003.

3 Smith, Bernie. <u>The Joy of Trivia</u>. New York: Bell Publishing Company, 1976, page 4 and 168.

4 Angelo, Joseph A, Jr. <u>Encyclopedia of Space and Astronomy</u>. New York: Facts on File, Inc., 2006.

5 Clark, Stuart. <u>Stars and Atoms: From the Big Bang to the Solar System</u>. New York: Oxford University Press, 2003.

6 Angelo, Joseph A, Jr. <u>Encyclopedia of Space and Astronomy</u>. New York: Facts on File, Inc., 2006.

7 Clark, Stuart. <u>Stars and Atoms: From the Big Bang to the Solar System</u>. New York: Oxford University Press, 2003.

8 Angelo, Joseph A, Jr. <u>Encyclopedia of Space and Astronomy</u>. New York: Facts on File, Inc., 2006.

9 Clark, Stuart. <u>Stars and Atoms: From the Big Bang to the Solar System</u>. New York: Oxford University Press, 2003.

10 Angelo, Joseph A, Jr. <u>Encyclopedia of Space and Astronomy</u>. New York: Facts on File, Inc., 2006.

11 Clark, Stuart. <u>Stars and Atoms: From the Big Bang to the Solar System</u>. New York: Oxford University Press, 2003.

12 Angelo, Joseph A, Jr. <u>Encyclopedia of Space and Astronomy</u>. New York: Facts on File, Inc., 2006.

13 Clark, Stuart. <u>Stars and Atoms: From the Big Bang to the Solar System</u>. New York: Oxford University Press, 2003.

14 Angelo, Joseph A, Jr. <u>Encyclopedia of Space and Astronomy</u>. New York: Facts on File, Inc., 2006.

15 Clark, Stuart. <u>Stars and Atoms: From the Big Bang to the Solar System</u>. New York: Oxford University Press, 2003.

16 Angelo, Joseph A, Jr. <u>Encyclopedia of Space and Astronomy</u>. New York: Facts on File, Inc., 2006.

17 Clark, Stuart. <u>Stars and Atoms: From the Big Bang to the Solar System</u>. New York: Oxford University Press, 2003.

18 Angelo, Joseph A, Jr. <u>Encyclopedia of Space and Astronomy</u>. New York: Facts on File, Inc., 2006.

19 Clark, Stuart. <u>Stars and Atoms: From the Big Bang to the Solar System</u>. New York: Oxford University Press, 2003.

20 "The Origin of the Solar System". <u>Encyclopedia of the Solar System</u>.Elsevier, 2nd ed, 2007.

21 Ibid.

22 Ibid.

23 Ibid.

24 Anathema. "Shroud of False". <u>Alternative 4</u>. Peaceville Records, CDVILEM 73 620732, 2000.

25 Marsa, Linda. "She Thinks, He Thinks". Discover: The Brain. Spring 2007.

26 Marieb, Elaine N.<u>Essentials of Human Anatomy &</u>

Physiology. 9th ed. Pearson Education, Inc. 2009.
        27 Ibid.
        28 The Science of Sex Appeal. Discovery
Communications, LLC, 2008.
        29 Ibid.
        30 Ibid.
        31 Ibid.
        32 National Geographic: Incredible Human Machine.
Dir. Irwin Rosten. NGHT, Inc, 2007.
        33 Ibid.
        34 Ibid.
        35 Ibid.
        36 Ibid.
        37 Ibid.
        38 Ibid.
        39 Ibid.
        40 Marieb, Elaine N.Essentials of Human Anatomy &
Physiology. 9th ed. Pearson Education, Inc. 2009.
        41 National Geographic: Incredible Human Machine.
Dir. Irwin Rosten. NGHT, Inc, 2007.
        42 Ibid.
        43 Ibid.
        44 Myers, David G. Exploring Psychology Fifth
Edition in Modules. New York: Worth Publishers, 2003. page
69.
        45 Ibid.

Purpose Decay-
        Teleologically Thwarted Legacy:
        1 George Ritzer. The McDonaldization of Society.
Thousand Oakes: Pine Forge Press, 2000.

2 Myers, David G. Exploring Psychology Fifth Edition in Modules. New York: Worth Publishers, 2003. page 431.

3 Ibid. page 430.

4 Ibid. page 429.

5 Ibid.

6 Ibid.

7 Ibid.

8 Jones, Darryl. Horror: A Thematic History in Fiction and Film. London: Arnold, 2002. page 53.

9 Ibid.

10 Ibid.

11 Ibid.

12 Myers, David G. Exploring Psychology Fifth Edition in Modules. New York: Worth Publishers, 2003. page 479.

13 Ibid.

14 Ibid.

15 Ibid. page 480.

16 Ibid.

17 Ibid. page 481.

Dissonant Moral Architecture:

1 Fiero, Gloria K. The Humanistic Tradition: Prehistory to the Early Modern World. 4th Ed. New York: McGraw Hill. 2002. page 372.

2 "Indulgence". The New Encyclopaedia Britannica. 15th ed. vol 6. 2002.

3 Ibid.

4 Empires: The Medici, Godfathers of the Renaissance. Dir. Justin Hardy. PBS Home Video. Produced by Lion Television, 2003.

5 Hibbert, Christopher. The House of Medici: Its Rise

and Downfall. New York: William Morrow & Company, Inc., 1975. pages 215-229.

    6 Ibid.

    7 Ibid.

    8 Ibid.

    9 Empires: The Medici, Godfathers of the Renaissance. Dir. Justin Hardy. PBS Home Video. Produced by Lion Television, 2003.

    10 Ibid.

    11 Dee, D and D.P. Sheridan. "Index of Prohibited Books". The New Catholic Encyclopedia. 2nd Ed. The Gale Group Inc., 2003. page 391.

    12 Ibid.

    13 Ibid.

    14 Flexner, Stuart and Doris Flexner. The Pessimist's Guide to History. Quill, 2000. pages 47-48.

    15 Fiero, Gloria K. The Humanistic Tradition: Prehistory to the Early Modern World. 4th Ed. New York: McGraw Hill. 2002. page 351.

    16 Flexner, Stuart and Doris Flexner. The Pessimist's Guide to History. Quill, 2000. pages 47-48.

    17 Cline, Austin. "Christian Censorship of Harry Potter: Schools, Libraries, and Free Speech". About.com. Retrieved 10-08-2011.

    18 Ibid.

    19 Ibid.

    20 Ibid.

    21 Ibid.

    22 Stokstad, Marilyn. Art History. New York: Harry N. Abrams, Inc., 1995. page 326.

    23 Ibid. page 547.

    24 Ibid.

25 Ibid. page 557.

26 Grodecki, Louis. Gothic Architecture. New York: Harry N. Abrams, Inc., 1977. page 20.

27 The Complete Dictionary of Symbols. Duncan Baird Publishers, 2004.

28 Ibid.

29 Ibid.

30 Ibid.

31 Ibid.

32 Ibid.

33 Ibid.

34 Ibid.

35 Ibid.

36 Ibid.

37 Ibid.

38 Ibid.

39 Callahan, Tim. "The Triumph of Christianity". Skeptic.Millennium Press, Inc., 2001. vol. 8 No. 4, 82-85.

40 Ibid.

41 Ibid.

42 Ermatinger, James W. The Decline and Fall of the Roman Empire. Greenwood Press, 2004.

43 Ibid.

44 Ibid.

45 Ibid.

46 A Concise Introduction to World Religions. Oxford University Press, 2007. page 263.

47 Ibid.

48 Ibid.

49 O'Callaghan, Sean. The Compact Guide to World Religions. Lion Hudson, 2010.

50 Ibid.

51 Noss, David S. <u>A History of the World's Religions</u>. 12th Ed. Pearson Education, Inc., 2008. page 106.

52 Ibid.

53 O'Callaghan, Sean. <u>The Compact Guide to World Religions</u>. Lion Hudson, 2010.

54 Osborne, Richard. <u>Introducing Eastern Philosophy.</u> Icon Books Ltd, 2006. .pages 87-147

55 Ibid.

56 "Torah". <u>The Student's Encyclopedia of Judaism</u>. New York: New York University Press, 2004. page 346.

57 Ibid.

58 "Christianity". <u>The New Encyclopaedia Britannica</u>. 15th ed. vol 16. 2002.

59 Ibid.

60 Ibid.

61 "Voodoo". <u>The New Encyclopaedia Britannica</u>. 15th ed. vol 12. 2002.

62 "Rastafarian". <u>The New Encyclopaedia Britannica</u>. 15th ed. vol 9. 2002.

63 Ibid.

64 "The Prophet, the Revelation, and the Founding of Islam". <u>The Muslim Almanac</u>. Gale Research Inc., 1996.

65 Ibid.

66 Ibid.

67 Ibid.

68 Cunningham, Scott. <u>Wicca: A Guide for the Solitary Practitioner</u>. Llewellyn Publications, 2004

69 LaVey, Anton Szandor. <u>The Satanic Bible</u>. New York: Avon Books, 1969.

70 Ibid.

71 Cunningham, Scott. <u>Wicca: A Guide for the Solitary Practitioner</u>. Llewellyn Publications, 2004

72 Reece, Gregory L. <u>UFO Religion:Inside Flying Saucer Cults and Culture</u>. New York: I.B. Tauris & Co Ltd, 2007. pages 182-186.

73 Ibid.

74 Ibid.

75 Ibid.

76 Ibid.

77 Henderson, Bobby. <u>The Gospel of the Flying Speghetti Monster</u>. New York: Villard Books, 2006.

78 Ibid.

79 Ibid.

80 Ibid.

81 Abel, Andrew Stuart and Andrew Schaefer. "Seeing Through the Invisible Pink Unicorn". Journal of Religion and Society. The Kripke Center, vol 12, 2010. ISSN: 1522-5658

82 Ibid.

83 Ibid.

84 Ibid.

85 Ibid.

86 Dawkins, Richard. <u>The God Delusion</u>.New York: First Mariner Books, 2006. pages 74-76.

87 Velasquez, Manuel. <u>Philosophy: A Text with Readings</u>. Wadsworth Group, 2002. page 283-299.

88 Ibid.

89 Ibid.

90 Ingram, David Bruce and Jennifer A. Parks. <u>The Complete Idiot's Guide to Understanding Ethics</u>. Alpha Books, 2002. pages 38-45.

91 Ibid.

92 Fredrich Nietzsche. <u>Twilight of the Idols/ The Anti-Christ</u>. Trans. R. J. Hollingdale. Penguin Books, 1968.

The Evolved Predator Mechanisms that Usurp:

1 Myers, David G. <u>Exploring Psychology Fifth Edition in Modules</u>. New York: Worth Publishers, 2003. page 248.

2 Ibid. page 353

3 Bearden, William O., Thomas N. Ingram, Raymond W. LaForge. <u>Marketing: Principles and Perspectives</u>. 4th ed.. New York: McGraw-Hill Companies, Inc., 2004. p.324-325.

4 Lempert, Philip. <u>Being the Shopper: Understanding the Buyer's Choice</u>. New York: John Wiley & Sons, Inc., 2002. p. 159.

5 Ibid. page 151.

6 Ibid.

7 Ibid. page 152.

8 Ibid. page 33.

9 Ibid. page 165.

10 Bearden, William O., Thomas N. Ingram, Raymond W. LaForge. <u>Marketing: Principles and Perspectives</u>. 4th ed.. New York: McGraw-Hill Companies, Inc., 2004. page 189.

11 Schlosser, Eric. <u>Fast Food Nation: the Dark Side of the All-American Meal</u>. New York: Houghton Mifflin, 2002. page 43.

12 Ibid.

13 Bearden, William O., Thomas N. Ingram, Raymond W. LaForge. <u>Marketing: Principles and Perspectives</u>. 4th ed.. New York: McGraw-Hill Companies, Inc., 2004. page 6.

14 Myers, David G. Exploring Psychology Fifth Edition in Modules. New York: Worth Publishers, 2003. pages 224-225.

15 Miller, Richard Lawrence. " Nicotine". The Encyclopedia of Addictive Drugs. Greenwood Press, 2002. pages 318-322.

16 Ibid.

17 Myers, David G. Exploring Psychology Fifth Edition in Modules. New York: Worth Publishers, 2003. pages 224-225.

18 Ibid.

19 Miller, Richard Lawrence. " Nicotine". The Encyclopedia of Addictive Drugs. Greenwood Press, 2002. pages 318-322.

20 Myers, David G. Exploring Psychology Fifth Edition in Modules. New York: Worth Publishers, 2003. pages 204.

21 Ibid.

22 Schlosser, Eric. Fast Food Nation: the Dark Side of the All-American Meal. New York: Houghton Mifflin, 2002. page 120.

23 Ibid. page 53.

24 Myers, David G. Exploring Psychology Fifth Edition in Modules. New York: Worth Publishers, 2003. pages 366.

25 Ibid. page 361.

26 Ibid. page 366.

27 Schlosser, Eric. Fast Food Nation: the Dark Side of the All-American Meal. New York: Houghton Mifflin, 2002. page 240.

28 Weapon: A Visual History of Arms and Armor. New York: DK Publishing, 2006. pages 276-277.

29 Ibid.

30 "War, Technology of". <u>The New Encyclopaedia Britannica</u>. 15th ed. vol 29. page 602.

31 Ibid. page 617.

32 Ibid.

33 Ibid. page 575.

34 Ibid.

35 Hedges, Chris. <u>What Every Person Should Know About War</u>. Free Press, 2003. pages 4 and 5.

36 Ibid.

37 Ibid.

38 Ibid.

39 Colorado Revised Statute 18-1-704

40 Ibid.

Nascent Omniscience-
Utopian Insights & Further Questioning:

1 Tzu, Lao. <u>Tao te Ching</u>. Trans. Stephen Mitchell. HarperCollins Publishers, 1988. page 76.

2 Velasquez, Manuel. <u>Philosophy: A Text with Readings</u>. Wadsworth Group, 2002. page 323.

3 Boss, Judith A. <u>Analyzing Moral Issues</u>. 3rd ed. New York: McGraw-Hill, 2005. pages 36-38.

4 "Population". <u>The New Encyclopaedia Britannica</u>. 15th ed. vol 25. page 1041.

5 <u>National Geographic: Collapse</u>. Dir. Noel Dockstader. NGHT, LLC. 2010.

6 <u>The Ecological Footprint: Accounting for a Small Planet</u>. Dir. Patsy Northcutt. With Mathis Wackernagel. Bullfrog Films, 2005.

7 Ibid.

8 Myers, David G. <u>Exploring Psychology Fifth Edition in Modules</u>. New York: Worth Publishers, 2003. page 430.

9 Alder, Vera Stanley. <u>The Finding of the Third Eye</u>. Samuel Weiser, Inc., 1968. pages 93-94.

10 Ibid.

11 Ibid.

12 Ibid.

13 Dawkins, Richard. <u>The God Delusion</u>.New York: First Mariner Books, 2006. pages 162-171.

14 <u>Vanishing of the Bees</u>. Directed by George Langworthy and Maryam Henein. Long Live the Queen, LLC, 2010.

15 Kaku, Michio. "The Physics of Interstellar Travel: To one day, reach the stars." Welcome to Explorations in Science with Dr. Michio Kaku at http://mkaku.org/home/ . Retrieved 2011-10-01.

16 Ibid.

17 Ibid.

18 Ibid.

- I n d e x -

activation-synthesis theory; 15

afterlife; 36-37

All Saints Church of Sedlec; 4

anatomy; 53-58

anthropic principle; 128

Aristotle; 117

art;
    as concept, 10
    Byzantine, 82
    Gothic style, 82-83

atmospherics; 104

atoms; 16, 51-52

beauty myth; 24-25, 53

brand loyalty; 105-106

breathing; 125-126

Buddhism; 88

"carpe diem types"; 121

castle doctrine; 112

Christianity; 76-78, 81-86, 90, 96-99

Confucius; 117
    Confucianism, 88

cosmology; 49-52

culture;
    definition, 19
    norms, 33
    origins, 20

dating; 54-55, 73

Dawkins, Richard; 22

Diamond, Jared; 12, 122

drive reduction theory; 103

ecological footprint; 123

ego(see also self); 40, 43, 47

Emerson, Ralph Waldo; 75

"Emotional-Social Intrigue of Nostalgia; 31

The Enlightenment; 11, 122

ethnocentrism; 19

fear; 13, 65-66

feminism; 26-28

Flying Spaghetti Monster; 91-92

Frankl, Viktor E; 38-39

Freud, Sigmund; 15, 93

geologic time; 10

God; 15, 95, 98
    arguments, 93
    divine command theory, 94
    to play, 115

goldilocks zones; 128

Harry Potter; 80-81

hedonism; 18, 107, 120

Hinduism; 88

holidays; 10

Index Librorum Prohibitorum; 79-80

individualism; 67-68

"Individualist Paradigm"; 60-62

indulgences; 77-78

Invisible Pink Unicorn; 92-93

Islam; 90

"Jenga Effect"; 34

Judaism; 22-23, 89
Kardashev, Nikolai;
    Kardashev Scale, 130
Life After People; 46
love; 73-74
Machiavelli, Niccolo; 38
Make My Day law; 113-114
masks; 41-42
The Matrix; 1
McDonaldization(see also
    George Ritzer); 62,
108
meaning;
    Logotherapy(see also
      Viktor E. Frankl),
        38-39
    reason; 12, 38
medicine; 47
names(see also
    nomenclature); 30
Nietzsche, Friedrich; 49, 98
nomenclature; 10
nucleosynthesis; 51
Old Testament; 22
operant conditioning; 103
pacificism; 111-112, 131
pan-behavioral deterministic
    nurture; 40-41
pets; 31-32
plague; 80
prajna; 120
redundancy; 8, 35-36, 44
Rastafari; 89-90
religion;
    six dimensions, 15
    origins, 21

teaching, 68
    variations, 77, 87-93
Ritzer, George; 62
Russell, Bertrand; 93
Satanism; 90-91
Schlosser, Eric; 110
Scientology; 91
self(see also ego); 13-14
seven wonders of the ancient
    world; 44-45
sex; 70-72
sexism;
    origins, 25-26
smoking; 107-108
Sophocles; 119
stress; 63-64, 109, 125
symbols; 83-85
syncretism; 83
Tainter, Joseph A; 122
Taoism; 88, 120
    Lao-tzu, 60
taxonomic rank; 10
technophobia, 65
television; 64-65
"Temporary Fix Effect"; 34
"Ultimate Paradox"; 61, 67
Vanishing of the Bees; 128
Voltaire; 75
weapons; 101, 110
Wicca; 90-91
Zoroaster;
    Zoroastrianism; 22-23